U.S. BUSINESS INVOLVEMENT IN EASTERN EUROPE

U.S. BUSINESS INVOLVEMENT IN EASTERN EUROPE

Case Studies of Hungary, Poland, and Romania

Martin Schnitzer

PRAEGER

PRAEGER SPECIAL STUDIES • PRAEGER SCIENTIFIC

Library of Congress Cataloging in Publication Data

Schnitzer, Martin.
  U.S. business involvement in Eastern Europe.

  Bibliography: p.
  Includes index.
  1. East-West trade (1945-   )--Case studies.
2. United States--Foreign economic relations--Europe,
Eastern--Case studies. 3. Europe, Eastern--Foriegn
economic relations--United States--Case studies.
I. Title.
HF1411.S2993   337.73'0171'7   78-19794
ISBN 0-03-043026-7

Published in 1980 by Praeger Publishers
CBS Educational and Professional Publishing
A Division of CBS, Inc.
521 Fifth Avenue, New York, New York 10017 U.S.A.

© 1980 by Praeger Publishers

0123456789 145 987654321

81-8976

PREFACE

The purpose of this book is to examine U.S. business involvement in Eastern Europe, with emphasis placed on various types of industrial-cooperation agreements. Special attention is given to three Eastern countries with which the United States has had good commercial relations—Hungary, Poland, and Romania. These countries have been receptive to attracting Western firms to participate jointly in a number of cooperation agreements. They sponsor, at least to some degree, joint-equity arrangements between Western and socialist enterprises. So far, the success of these arrangements has been somewhat limited, and the future potential for U.S. and Western European business involvement in these countries appears to be restricted to a degree because of the increased indebtedness of the East to Western financial institutions and a shortage of hard currency. The potential for U.S. and Western business involvement varies from country to country and also depends upon priorities established in the economic plans of the Eastern European countries.

Much of the data used in the study was based upon sources obtained in Eastern Europe and from the Washington embassies of Hungary, Poland, and Romania. Reliance was placed upon mail questionnaires and interviews with executives of U.S. firms operating in Eastern Europe. The objective of the questionnaire approach was to obtain information concerning the future potential for U.S. business involvement in Eastern Europe and to catalog the various types of industrial-cooperation agreements in which U.S. business firms are involved. Responses to the mail questionnaire constitute the foundation for the concluding chapter. Other major sources of information include publications of the Joint Economic Committee of the U.S. Congress and the Bureau of East-West Trade of the U.S. Department of Commerce.

The author is especially indebted to the following persons who assisted him in obtaining the necessary information for the book: Christopher Ziemnowicz, of Warsaw Polytechnic University, who obtained much of the information on U.S. business involvement in Poland from Polish sources; Jay Burgess, Senior Romanian Desk Officer, Eastern European Affairs Division, U.S. Department of Commerce; Michael Hegedus, Senior Hungarian Desk Officer, Eastern European Affairs Division; Jenelle Matheson, Policy Analyst, Bureau of East-West Trade, U.S. Department of Commerce; and Findley A. Estlick, Vice-President, Foreign Assembly and Plant Facilities, Piper Aircraft.

CONTENTS

LIST OF TABLES

U.S. BUSINESS INVOLVEMENT IN EASTERN EUROPE

1
U. S. TRADE AND
THE EAST-WEST
ECONOMIC EVOLUTION

The purpose of this book is to explore the role of U.S. business firms in commercial contacts between the industrialized nations of the West and those nations of Eastern Europe, including the Soviet Union. [1] Special emphasis will be placed on newer forms of commercial relationships that have developed during the 1970s—relationships that come under the general category of industrial-cooperation agreements. These agreements represent a shift in the way business is being done between East and West, that is, the socialist and capitalist countries. Prior to the 1970s, East-West trade was characterized primarily by buying and selling, which involved straight export-import transactions. But as trade expanded, the forms of commercial relations between East and West also expanded and became more complex. A need developed for the East to alleviate its ever-increasing balance-of-payments deficit with the West and to compensate for its lack of investment capital. There was also a desire to expand and diversify individual national economies, to penetrate new markets, and to bridge an ever-widening technology gap with the West.

The problems that developed in Eastern Europe were to a large extent the result of an oversimplified approach to foreign-trade management and economic and industrial development. For a considerable period of time, industrial-development policy in the socialist countries emphasized the growth of a self-sufficient industrial base. This led to broad—but superficial, submarginal, and insufficiently specialized—industrial development. Stress was placed on import substitution rather than the promotion of manufacture based upon comparative advantage and efficient resource allocation. This approach slowed the evolution of domestic industry founded upon rational economic specialization and did not permit the early maturity of large-scale exports of specialized industrial production. Moreover, the small-scale

1

production of numerous products did not create a sufficient export supply potential. Most often, these products were of low value, low technical levels not up to world standards, and frequently not adaptable to the needs and requirements of foreign customers. Thus, an imbalance in socialist foreign trade developed, with imports exceeding exports, and this led to balance-of-payments problems.

Industrial cooperation between East and West developed as a result of these socialist economic problems. Western firms have become involved in numerous industrial-cooperation agreements with the East. These agreements are defined by one writer as arrangements whereby individual producers, based in East and West, pool some assets and coordinate their use in the mutual pursuit of complementary objectives.[2] U.S. firms have not been as actively involved as other Western firms in participating in these agreements, but the interest is there. Three Eastern European countries offer some attraction to U.S. firms for reasons that are explained below. These countries are Poland, Hungary, and Romania. The U.S. business presence in each of these countries will be the subject of Chapters 4, 5, and 6, respectively.

The political situation in Poland, particularly vis-à-vis the United States, is relatively favorable to industrial-cooperation arrangements between U.S. business firms and Polish state enterprises. Even before the visit of Richard Nixon in 1972, Poland was a member of the General Agreement on Tariffs and Trade, had been granted most-favored-nation (MFN) status by the United States, and had been treated more leniently than its socialist neighbors by U.S. export control regulations. The Nixon visit and a subsequent visit to Washington by Polish Premier Edward Gierek resulted in a series of agreements that improved the already favorable business and commercial relations between the two countries. Export-Import Bank (Eximbank) credits were extended to include trade with Poland, with a reciprocal extension of credit by the Polish State Bank Handlowy w Warszawicz. Permission was granted to U.S. business firms to seek licenses for operating commercial representations in Poland, and a U.S. Trade Development Information Office was opened in Warsaw. Poland expressed strong interest in undertaking joint ventures in industrial cooperation with U.S. firms. During the 1970s the U.S. share of Western industrial-cooperation agreements with Poland showed a considerable increase, reflecting an increased interest on the part of U.S. business firms in Poland.

U.S. relations with Romania have also been generally good. President Nixon's visit to Romania in August 1969 was the first by a U.S. president to a Warsaw Pact country. In April 1971 the U.S. secretary of commerce visited Romania with the subsequent result that the country was made eligible for Eximbank credits. Romania was also granted MFN treatment with respect to exports to the United States. In turn Romania took a number of steps to expand and facilitate trade with the Western world. It became the first socialist country to join the International Monetary Fund and the International Bank for Reconstruction and Development. Of more practical importance to U.S. business firms were Romanian measures designed to make their country more accessible to foreign firms, culminating in the Romanian laws and regulations of 1971 and 1972 permitting the formulation of joint ventures with foreign firms and the decree of 1971, which allows foreign firms to establish their own offices in Romania. In 1973 the visit of Romanian President Nicolae Ceauşescu to the United States resulted in the creation of a bilateral U.S.-Romanian Economic Commission.

Hungary has been the most active of the Eastern European countries in seeking and concluding industrial-cooperation agreements with Western firms. This can be attributed to economic and political reforms that have given Hungary an economic system significantly different from the other countries of Eastern Europe, combining state ownership of the means of production with economic planning but lacking the command system of allocation used to implement the plans elsewhere. Instead, the plan was to be the framework for a "guided market" allocation system in which the economy would be run on a profit-based incentive system for enterprises. Industrial cooperation with the West was a part of overall Hungarian economic policy in which, among other things, the Hungarian economy was to be adapted to changing conditions of the international division of labor. Cooperation with Western firms was seen as a means to stimulate greater efficiency and productivity in Hungarian enterprises. Industrial-cooperation agreements are used to gain access for Hungarian exports in Western markets and to provide a substitute for imports through the cooperative delivery of end-use products.

THE EAST-WEST ECONOMIC EVOLUTION

The current, but fragile, trend toward closer economic cooperation between the capitalist and socialist countries is the result of a number of political and economic factors that have materialized primarily in the last decade. Probably the most important factor was the easing of worldwide political tensions between East and West in the late 1960s and early 1970s. Détente brought about a change in attitudes on the part of both the capitalist and socialist countries. Much of the easing of restrictions by the capitalist countries, in particular the United States, has been based on the premise that closer economic ties between East and West will lead to a decrease in political tensions. The socialist countries have reached a point in economic development where progress has to be brought about by using their plants and labor more efficiently. A move from an extensive to an intensive economic development has required new technology, industrial efficiency, and a hard-currency market and, of necessity, has precipitated a number of economic reforms within the socialist countries.

Economic Reforms

To improve economic efficiency, a series of reforms was instituted by the socialist countries, especially during the late 1960s. The significant elements of these reforms involved a number of areas. State industrial enterprises were given greater freedom to choose ways and means of plan fulfillment. Profit was accepted as the main indicator of state-enterprise performance, while the total number of success indicators was reduced drastically. Increased importance was attached to material, as distinct from moral, incentives. Planning was made less prescriptive and detailed; instead, efforts were made to lay down broad targets expressed in value terms. Prices were brought more in line with production costs to reduce the need for state subsidies and to enable the typical state enterprise to be profitable. Similarly, procurement prices paid to state and collective farms were raised in relation to industrial prices to increase agricultural production and to improve living standards in rural areas. There was some overhaul of the retail and wholesale trade network, designed to improve services to consumers and to enable effective transmission of customers' preferences to producing enterprises.

These reforms were by no means uniform in all of the socialist countries. Yugoslavia, which has remained free from Soviet influence, has had more latitude in terms of reform action. The purpose of the Yugoslav economic reforms has been to develop a decentralized economic system—in part, for political reasons and, in part, to promote economic efficiency. The other socialist countries, within the limits of Soviet tolerance, were able to pursue different policy lines. The policies that were implemented by the countries were related to their perception of economic performance and requirements. Romania was less inclined than the other socialist countries to vary from Stalinist economic institutions in that priority was given to the development of heavy industry. On the other hand, economic reforms in Czechoslovakia, Hungary, and East Germany took the form of changes in price policies. Each country adopted a multiple-price system, with some prices free, other prices varied within limits, and some prices fixed. Production criteria of total quantity output at the enterprise level were replaced by monetary and qualitative criteria such as sales, costs, and profits.

The reform movement in Eastern Europe emerged because of general dissatisfaction with the nature and result of the traditional Soviet-type economic system installed in the area after World War II. However, there has been a general retreat from reform, the extent of the retreat varying from country to country. Changes in administrative organization, planning methods, performance indicators, and incentives created the opposition of special interest groups. There was an ambivalent attitude on the part of Communist party leaders, who feared a lessening of their authority and control. Caution and delay were often involved in the implementation of the reforms. The state was ready to take away what it had given at the first sign of real independence. In Hungary, for example, enterprises and individuals discovered that indirect regulators and controls exercised by the state provided constraints that manipulated the market framework.[3] Moreover, there were no political reforms to accompany decentralization of economic decision making at the enterprise level. Although there was an effort to achieve decentralization of decision making, there was no corresponding effort to provide more autonomy in terms of political rights. All economic decisions have had to be made within the constraints of a highly circumscribed political framework. Inevitably, the reforms have come into conflict with ideological and political issues.

Problems of unsatisfactory growth rates, balance-of-payments difficulties, and lagging technological progress continue to be pervasive in the Soviet Union and Eastern Europe. The proliferation of economic claimants for goods and services runs well ahead of the ability of the output increases to satisfy demands. Options for improved performance are somewhat limited, and the mixture of costs and benefits is somewhat complex. Investment resources are not easily shifted from defense and export industries to modernize and expand consumer-related activities. Likewise, modest economic growth limits the incremental resource supply to be shared among the various resource claimants. In their search for corrective ways other than changes in the economic mechanism, the Eastern European countries have turned their attention to foreign trade and investment.

Rising Living Standards

Consumers in the Soviet Union and Eastern Europe have long paid the price for rapid industrialization and economic growth. There have always been shortages in the production of consumer goods, for top priority was assigned to the development of the capital goods industries. Resource allocation went into the production of capital goods, the procreative element in economic growth. This, however, has been subject to some change, because socialist consumers have come to want a higher standard of living now rather than at some unspecified time in a Communist utopia of the future. Although there is no question that consumers' standard of living has improved rather dramatically, particularly since 1970, both the quantity and quality of consumer goods still leave much to be desired. The speed with which new products and new production methods are introduced remains unsatisfactory. After three decades of socialist rule, the supply of many goods and services remains limited. Standing in line, waiting years for cars and apartments, searching the shops for scarce products, and bribing the butcher and the repairman are a way of life for socialist consumers. For the many families in which all adults work, often moonlighting as well, there is never enough time to shop.

The automobile, a ubiquitous symbol of high living standards in the West, is in short supply in the Soviet Union and Eastern Europe. To some extent production of automobiles is circumscribed by a lack of good roads and repair facilities. However, the socialist countries have found it very difficult to independently produce such highly complex products as motor vehicles on an economic scale. Moreover, few of the vehicles are competitive in world markets. Car prices are high and quality is low by Western standards. Necessary production equipment, common vendor-supplied parts, and broadly diversified supporting industry are not available in the socialist countries. Despite some experience in mass producing motor vehicles, particularly trucks, the Soviet Union only recently began a serious program to expand the output of modern automotive production equipment. The Soviet Union does not have the capacity to provide automotive items to Eastern European countries, and feelings of national sovereignty have kept individual countries from supporting the role of the Council for Mutual Economic Assistance (CMEA), as an instrument to guide and coordinate the development of an integrated regional industry.

Problems of Agriculture

An increase in population and a rise in per capita income have combined to generate a constantly increasing demand for an improved product mix in the socialist countries. However, there have been perennial problems of inefficiency, low labor productivity, and high production costs associated with socialist agriculture. Despite the fact that agriculture has received a high priority in the five-year plans and the economic reforms of the socialist countries, farm productivity lags far behind productivity in industry. Emphasis on mechanization and material incentives to stimulate farm output has not yielded the desired results. The end result of general agricultural inefficiency is that the socialist countries are among the most expensive food producers in the world, a fact that redounds to the disadvantage of the consumer because real income is reduced in comparison with that in other countries. There have been meat shortages in Poland and the Soviet Union. The need developed in the socialist countries to import agricultural products, including farm machinery, from Western sources. For the 1972-76 period, agricultural products accounted for nearly 74 percent of U.S. exports to the socialist countries as a whole.

Persistently unsatisfactory performance in agriculture has directed increased policy efforts by the socialist countries toward potential gains from expanded and improved participation in the international division of labor. Agricultural products from the West have increased in terms of demand. In 1976, for example, agricultural products represented around 60 percent of total U.S. exports to the Soviet Union and 70 percent of U.S. exports to Poland. Wheat and corn exports are of particular importance and reflect contractual agreements made between the United States and the two socialist countries. While the total value of wheat and corn sales is large, accounting for $1.5 billion in exports to the Soviet Union and Poland, they account for a small portion of U.S. grain production. Wheat sales to the Soviet Union and Poland represented less than 8 percent of total U.S. grain production in 1976, and corn production represented less than 3 percent of total U.S. production. Viewed another way, wheat and corn sales to the two most important socialist importers of U.S. products represented 13 percent of total U.S. wheat and corn exports to the world markets in 1976.

Other Factors

Recent developments in the socialist economies of Eastern Europe have created an environment for favorable industrial cooperation between East and West. Mounting problems in the economic systems of the socialist countries have exacerbated many economic deficiencies. Extensive economic development brought out costly and widespread industrial inefficiency and labor shortages. The development plans of the socialist countries called for a move from extensive to intensive economic growth, a departure from promoting growth through the addition of new plants and increases in the labor force to promoting it through a more efficient utilization of existing plants and labor. One of the problems faced by the socialist countries has been that their economic development was being hampered by a lack of sophisticated technology in most fields. Such technology became necessary in order to utilize existing resources more efficiently, and the socialist countries turned to the West for the importation of this technology.

Imports of technology, however, placed a heavy financial burden on the economies of the Eastern European countries, which was compounded by a limited access to hard currency. Most of the foreign trade of the Eastern European countries takes place within the framework of the CMEA and thus does not generate the hard currency necessary to do business with the West. In many situations this inability to earn hard currency is attributable to the fact that most socialist state enterprises are unable to offer products or services that are up to the quality standards found in the highly competitive world markets. Another limiting factor has been the inadequate international marketing expertise of state enterprises and foreign-trade organizations. The disintegration of stable markets and prices has further hampered the economies of the socialist countries. This has assumed critical proportions as the higher import prices they are forced to pay are not duplicated by higher prices for exports because of their marginal position in the world markets.

Operating under these conditions, the socialist countries have two alternatives—to reduce economic growth or to explore new markets. The latter involves the development of new types of economic ties to the capitalist countries. During the early 1970s an environment was created whereby the governments of the socialist countries and managers of Western firms have realized opportunities for various new forms of joint business ventures. The easing of worldwide tensions permitted development of less-rigid views and greater exchange of data between East and West. However, the relations between East and West depend to a considerable degree on the existence of good relations between the United States and the Soviet Union. These relations are currently strained. By linking civil rights to MFN status for the Soviet Union, a limitation is set on the availability of U.S. credit for East-West trade.

Market Potential for Western Business Firms

The market potential of the socialist countries for Western products is considerable. There has been a change from an extensive to an intensive economic growth strategy requiring sophisticated technology and industrial equipment developed and marketed for the most part by Western multinational corporations. Higher standards of living and rising consumer expectations have resulted in dissatisfaction with product assortments produced by domestic manufacturers. The

TABLE 1

Economic and Demographic Data for the Eastern European
Socialist Countries, 1975

Country	Population (millions)	National Income (billions of dollars)	Five-Year Increase (constant prices, in percent)	Per Capita (dollars)
Bulgaria	8.7	14.7	42.0	1,690
Czechoslovakia	14.8	40.6	30.5	2,741
German Democratic Republic	16.8	55.5	30.3	3,295
Hungary	10.5	18.7	35.4	1,776
Poland	34.0	65.6	46.4	1,929
Romania	21.2	56.2	59.1	2,650
Soviet Union	254.4	486.5	25.6	1,912

Source: Business International, "Indicators of Market Size for 132 Countries," 1977 rep. ed., December 3, 10, 17, 24, 1976.

socialist countries, as a group, have a relatively high income and a large share of world output in comparison with Latin America and Africa. Table 1 represents a breakdown of demographic and economic data for the Soviet Union and the Eastern European region for 1975. As a region the rate of economic growth was superior to that of Western Europe for the period 1971-75, even though a sizable difference in per capita income continues to exist.

U.S. INVOLVEMENT IN EAST-WEST TRADE

The U.S. role in East-West trade has been small when compared with other highly industrialized capitalist nations, particularly Japan and West Germany. In 1973, for example, the United States had only 3.5 percent of the total market shares of manufactured goods exported to the socialist countries, compared with 40.9 percent for West Germany and 7.5 percent for Japan. However, there has been a transition from a passive to a more active U.S. role in East-West

TABLE 2

Total Trade Turnover between the United States and the Socialist
Countries, 1976
(millions of dollars)

Country	Exports	Imports	Turnover
Bulgaria	43.2	26.4	69.6
Czechoslovakia	148.8	36.0	184.8
German Democratic Republic	64.8	13.2	78.0
Hungary	63.6	49.2	112.8
Poland	624.0	319.2	943.2
Romania	249.6	199.2	448.8
Soviet Union	2,307.6	220.8	2,528.4
Total	3,501.6	864.0	4,365.6

Sources: Organization for Economic Cooperation and Development, Statistics of Foreign Trade, May 1977, p. 2; Federal Republic
of Germany, Statistiches Bundesamt, Gross und Einzelhanden, Series
6 (December 1976), pp. 1-3.

trade, dictated in part by increased world business competition. In
1976 the U.S. share of the export market for manufactured goods to
the socialist countries was 5.1 percent, and the U.S. share of the export market for all goods, including agricultural products, amounted
to 12.2 percent. But it is necessary to emphasize the U.S. involvement in East-West trade could very easily take a turn for the worse.
Trade with the socialist countries has been somewhat of a controversial issue in the United States. Unless this controversy and the policies that grew out of it can be resolved, many significant trading opportunities and markets for U.S. goods may be lost.

Table 2 presents the total volume of trade turnover between the
United States and the Soviet Union and the satellite countries of Eastern Europe for 1976. There is considerable imbalance between exports and imports, with the United States having a favorable trade
balance of $2.6 billion for the year. Of particular importance is the
volume of trade with Poland and Romania. Trade with Poland can be
expected to increase, at least at a moderate rate, since that country
now receives nondiscriminating tariff treatment, is eligible for Eximbank and Commodity Credit Corporation credits, has large deposits

of natural resources that enhance its hard-currency capabilities, and has set specific targets for expansion of trade with the United States. Romania, like Poland, is anxious to improve its commercial ties with the United States and to improve its industrial capabilities by imports of U.S. goods and services.

U.S. Exports to the Socialist Countries

Agricultural products account for the bulk of U.S. exports to the socialist countries. These exports produce the same balance-of-trade benefits as exports of manufactured goods and have similar beneficial employment effects. Sales of agricultural goods can be expected to remain the mainstay of U.S. exports to the socialist countries for some time to come, particularly given the problems of socialist agriculture.[4] With diplomatic relations initiated between the United States and the People's Republic of China, a new market for U.S. agricultural products has been opened. But the ability of the United States to sell large volumes of agricultural products to the socialist countries has created some controversy, for it is felt that the Soviets have been able to purchase grain at prices detrimental to the interests of the U.S. consumer and the U.S. farmer.

The performance of the United States in the sale of manufactured goods to the socialist countries lags far behind that of Western Europe and Japan. In 1976, 73 percent of all exports of the Western countries to the socialist countries were manufactured goods. The United States ranked tenth among the Western countries in manufacturing exports, ranking behind Belgium and Sweden.[5] The U.S. share of manufacturing exports is well below its competitive potential, because it supplied 16 percent of Western exports of manufactured goods in 1976. U.S.-manufacturing exports to the socialist countries consist primarily of such products as machine tools and equipment, pumps and compressors, aircraft and parts, automotive manufacturing equipment, and electrical machinery. The leading customer is the Soviet Union, with one-half of the total purchases of U.S.-manufacturing exports. U.S. firms have sold equipment to be used in the development of Soviet Siberia and other underdeveloped areas, and in view of the fact that Soviet officials have announced that large industrial and housing projects will be located in these areas, sales of U.S.-manufactured goods could increase significantly. The projects are of such dimensions that large inputs of Western equipment will be needed.

Exports to the other socialist countries vary in importance, with Poland and Romania being the most important customers. The total volume of U.S. exports to Poland is largely a function of the generally increasing volume of Polish grain exports from the United States. However, continuing pressure for more consumer goods, as well as the decision of the Polish government to give that sector priority, should increase the sale of U.S.-manufactured goods. U.S. exports to Romania doubled during the 1972-76 period, and the Romanian industrial sectors most heavily targeted for growth over the 1976-80 plan period are machine building, chemicals, and petrochemicals. As part of its economic development program, Romania is emphasizing cooperative activities with other countries, including the United States. Exports to Czechoslovakia have also increased, and this country intends to buy $3.5 billion of machinery and equipment in the West during the 1976-80 plan period, as it seeks the latest technology to update industrial processes. Exports to the German Democratic Republic, the most sophisticated of the socialist countries in terms of living standards, may increase with the establishment of diplomatic relations with the United States. Exports to Hungary, although unimportant at present, could increase, as this country plans to spend $6 to $8 billion for purchases of machinery and equipment during the 1976-80 plan period.

U.S. Imports from the Socialist Countries

Imports from the socialist countries are either raw materials or low-technology manufactured goods. In 1976, 94 percent of U.S. imports from the Soviet Union were in the category of industrial supplies and materials.[6] Included in this category are fuels and lubricants, paper and paper-base stocks, textile supplies and materials, industrial chemicals, lumber and other unfinished building materials, and nonmetals associated with durable-goods output. Imports of capital goods accounted for less than 1 percent of U.S. imports from the Soviet Union. One import from the Soviet Union that is of increasing importance is platinum, a metal used in the catalytic converter required in all U.S. automobiles manufactured after 1977. Given the enormous natural resources of the Soviet Union—particularly petroleum and natural gas resources in which the United States is deficient —imports from the Soviet Union can be expected to increase in the future. This assumes, of course, that reasonably good political relations between the two countries continue. There is the need in the Soviet home market, and it is apparent that the Soviets will have to rely on exports of raw materials to the United States to earn currency to pay for consumer goods.

Imports from Poland and Romania are balanced between agricultural and manufactured goods. The United States imported around $150 million in agricultural products from Poland in 1976.[7] The most important import is canned hams and pork, accounting for 88 percent of agricultural imports. Imports of manufactured goods consisted of leather footwear, organic chemicals, iron and steel sheets, and iron and steel nails. U.S. imports from Romania are concentrated in two areas—mineral fuels and manufactured articles. Agricultural imports involve canned hams, pork, and cheese. Both Poland and Romania have MFN agreements with the United States. This benefits their exports to the United States, because the United States tends to import large quantities of processed and semiprocessed raw materials. Since these are subject to high non-MFN tariff rates, Polish and Romanian products benefit. It can be assumed that both countries will make an increased effort to export manufactured products as well as raw and semiprocessed materials to the United States.

There is an imbalance between U.S. exports to and imports from the socialist countries. In 1976, for example, U.S. exports to the Soviet Union amounted to $2.3 billion, but imports were only $210 million. This imbalance also existed with the other socialist countries. For the most part U.S. imports from the socialist countries are raw material items essential for industry. U.S. exports are primarily agricultural, but a dollar's worth of agricultural exports has the same balance-of-trade benefits as a dollar derived from the export of manufactured goods and also has beneficial employment effects. However, the problem of foreign trade is not with the United States but with the socialist countries, for their trade imbalance is negative, with a drain on their currencies to pay for U.S. imports. A continued expansion of trade between the United States and the socialist countries requires more U.S. absorption of socialist exports if these countries are to be able to pay for their imports.

Factors Concerning the U.S. Role
in East-West Trade

The United States is in a disadvantaged position in East-West trade because of its late start. Trading relations between Western European and Japanese business firms and their counterparts in the Soviet Union and the other socialist countries have long been established, and it is difficult for the United States to gain an equal footing. The socialist countries are a group of nations whose population is about one-third of the world's total, who occupy 25 percent of the earth's surface, and who own much of the mineral wealth of the world. Western nations are eager to trade with the socialist countries and generally do not overtly attempt to use their trade to extract political and other concessions. No nation is self-sufficient in the raw materials and foods it requires to feed its industries and its people nor

in the advanced technologies that are vital to the most efficient production of goods and services. This applies to the United States, for
to neglect the socialist countries is to leave their markets open to the
Germans, Japanese, and other world competitors.

Nevertheless, there are certain factors involving the U.S. role
in East-West trade that need to be explored. One factor that has an
effect on both U.S. exports and imports is the economic planning of
the socialist countries. Another factor is the use of discriminatory
tariffs against most of the socialist countries. A third factor involves
the use of political leverage to extract concessions from the socialist
countries in such areas as human rights. Another factor concerns
credit advancement to the socialist countries, but in particular the
Soviet Union. There is the concern that large amounts of U.S. funds
are used to finance exports to the Soviet Union, a concern that was a
contributing factor to the limitations on additional lending to the Soviet Union in the Export-Import Bank Amendments of 1974.[8]

Economic Planning

State economic planning is the method of deciding key economic
questions in socialist industry—for example, what, how much of each
item, and for whom to produce—and the allocation of resources necessary to achieve the desired production and distribution. Although socialist economies make use of a system of money and prices, the
prices of goods and services and those of agents of production are
not determined by the competition of buyers and sellers in the market
and hence are not reliable guides for making economic decisions. A
socialist economic system has the ability to make economic plans and
to see to it that these plans are carried out. This is because the productive wealth of the system, consisting of land and capital, is owned
by society as a whole, and society, as reflected through the state, is
the only business entrepreneur of any importance and controls most
lines of economic activity, including foreign trade. Both exports and
imports are determined by the national economic plan.

The Soviet Union and the other socialist countries of Eastern
Europe have formulated their five-year plans covering the 1976-80
period. Involved are decisions about the directions their economic
development will take, what lines of industry and services will be
emphasized, and, accordingly, what kinds of goods, machinery,
equipment, and technology are to be exported and imported during the
plan period. Therefore, trade with the socialist countries depends
upon the priorities set in the national economic plans. To maintain
control over foreign trade, state trading enterprises exist in each socialist country. The quantities and sources of exports and imports
are the responsibility of these enterprises. In doing business with

the socialist countries, U.S. firms have to be aware of the trade priorities established in the national economic plans. These priorities can be changed from time to time. In addition, U.S. business firms must deal with state trading enterprises rather than individual state firms.

Tariffs

With the exceptions of Poland, Hungary, and Romania, the United States does not extend MFN tariff treatment to the socialist countries. To some extent this discrimination presents an obstacle to the stated U.S. goal of seeking a normalization of commercial relations with the socialist world. The United States is the only capitalist country that does not extend MFN treatment to the socialist nations, and this is an economic issue with long-range importance. The reason for the discrimination is an imbalance in their balance of payments with the United States. Imports from the United States have exceeded exports to the United States, resulting in increased socialist indebtedness and a decline in their hard-currency position. In the final analysis, socialist indebtedness to the United States can only be reduced through increased exports. A continued expansion of U.S. foreign trade with the socialist countries requires some relaxation of tariffs if these countries are to be able to pay for their imports.

The economic effects of tariff discrimination vary among the socialist countries. Exports from the Soviet Union to the United States have been largely raw materials, which are relatively free from U.S. tariffs. However, U.S. tariff rates tend to escalate relative to the degree of processing, and Soviet exports have been changing in composition, reflecting a higher degree of processing in some items and greater emphasis on intermediate manufactures and some finished products. Other socialist countries are affected more adversely than the Soviet Union by high U.S. tariff rates. In 1970, for example, 73 percent of the U.S. imports from Czechoslovakia were subject to discriminating tariffs compared with 10 percent from the Soviet Union.[9] Failure to grant MFN treatment to the Soviet Union and other socialist countries could hamper U.S. access to valuable sources of such products as iron and steel, processed food, transportation equipment, and petroleum. National security and foreign policy benefits presumed to arise from U.S. denial of MFN treatment to the Soviet Union and other socialist countries are not persuasive arguments for tariff discrimination.

Political Leverage

There has been an attempt on the part of the United States to link trade and credit to the internal policies of the socialist countries.

The rationale of U.S. policy was to use credit as a leverage to compel the socialist countries, in particular the Soviet Union, to comply with U.S.-defined humanitarian goals. One issue involves the free emigration of Soviet Jews to Israel. The use of trade and finance leverage was involved in the Trade Act of 1974, which the Soviet Union opposed on the grounds that it was inconsistent with the 1972 U.S.-Soviet Commercial Agreement, which called for an unconditional elimination of discriminatory trade restrictions, and with the principle of noninterference in domestic affairs. The Soviet action was seen by many observers as a setback to détente, particularly as other socialist countries supported the Soviet line on the Trade Act. There is also a potential for the socialist countries to apply reverse leverage on the United States. Competitor Western nations are eager to trade with the socialist countries and generally do not overtly attempt to use their trade to extract political concessions. They would welcome any action taken by the United States that might curtail its ability to compete in Eastern markets.

Credit Policies

There has been a gradual acceptance by Western international financial institutions of the socialist countries as an area for loanable funds. These funds come from both private and public Western banking sources and are used to finance both short-term export transactions and long-term industrial development projects. Most loans to the socialist countries come from lending institutions located in the Western European countries and Japan; the extent of U.S. involvement in the supply of credit is relatively small. In 1974, for example, Soviet medium- and long-term debt to the West was $4.2 billion; of that total, U.S. commercial banks held $350 million.[10] Western credit to the Soviet Union generally falls into two categories: general lines of credit extended over a specific period of time to cover a broad range of capital goods sales and credits or credit lines granted on a case-by-case project basis. In a general line of credit agreement, Canada has made available up to $500 million in credits to finance Canadian exports to the Soviet Union. All of the credit has to be utilized within two years.

The two main U.S. sources for financing exports to the socialist countries are the Eximbank and the commercial banking system.[11] The role of Eximbank is to promote U.S. exports, and it does this by making direct loans to exporters and importers and by insuring and guaranteeing loans extended by private lenders. However, the role of Eximbank as a credit source for the socialist countries is circumscribed by law. At present Poland and Romania are the only Eastern European countries permitted to have Eximbank credit. Eximbank financing proved to be of importance in the development of joint U.S.-Soviet economic agreements to develop natural gas and raw materials in the Soviet Union. In 1973 there was an $86 million loan to the Soviet Union to construct a truck plant, a $22 million loan to Poland for two meat-packing plants, and a $20 million loan to Romania to purchase jet aircraft. These loans, of course, resulted in more business for U.S. firms because they are used to provide an incentive through low-cost financing for foreign buyers to purchase from U.S. suppliers.

Large U.S. commercial banks can also extend credit to the Eastern European countries. However, the commercial banks are limited in the amounts they can lend to a single borrower, both by legal restrictions and by their own standards. Federally chartered banks are restricted to lending a maximum of 10 percent of their gross capital funds to a single borrower. Because each socialist country borrows through its foreign-trade bank, each has been considered a single borrower. This effectively limits the amount that the U.S. banking system could have on loan at any one time to any one socialist country to a theoretical maximum of about $2 billion. But banks would never reach this theoretical maximum because there are usually more profitable alternative uses of the available capital in other markets, and individual bank limits on lending in a given country are lower than the maximum that could be legally loaned. These limits are the product of bankers' desire to diversify their risks, and they provide an effective barrier to any large volume of lending to a socialist country.

The inability of the United States to provide government-backed financing for export sales to the Eastern European countries other than Poland and Romania can provide a substantial obstacle to a full realization of the trade opportunities that exist in these countries. The other capitalist countries are able to extend a more complete line of credit, often backed by government guarantees, to the socialist countries. For example, the West German government provides commercial and political risk insurance on credits offered to the socialist countries by consortia of German private lending institutions. Another example is the large interest-free credit that West Germany provides to East Germany. The availability of credit is an important factor in deciding where major Eastern European purchases will be made. To be competitive a U.S. firm may be forced to produce its product in the plant of a European subsidiary in order to be eligible for government credits available there.

Debt of the Socialist Countries

The debt of the socialist countries is large, and it will continue to grow. Some concern has been expressed over the size of the debt, which was nearly $60 billion in 1977, owed by the Eastern European countries to the West on the grounds that a default could lead to a depression in the West. The size of the debt shows the dependence of the socialist countries upon the capitalist nations, which have had generations of capital formation. The balance-of-payments problems of the socialist countries created by an imbalance of imports over exports contributes to the debt problem. Imports from the capitalist countries have increased at a faster rate than exports to these countries, and the inflation prevalent in the capitalist countries has contributed to the balance-of-payments deficit, with a resulting drain on the hard currencies of the socialist countries. Although the socialist countries have had an excellent record of debt repayment, there are limits to the extent of credit that they can or are willing to obtain. To slow their trade imbalances, attempts have been made to decrease imports of Western products, while capital projects have also been reduced.

The accumulated Eastern European hard-currency indebtedness is about double the level of annual exports to the West. However, the extent of the indebtedness varies from country to country. Poland and Romania, with the most abundant raw materials in Eastern Europe exclusive of the Soviet Union, started out in the best position to avoid large deficits with the developed West. But they have been correspondingly more ambitious in planning economic growth and creating large capital projects. The result has been an increase in their hard-currency indebtedness—Poland's indebtedness to the West increasing from $6.9 billion in 1975 to $10.0 billion in 1976 and Romania's indebtedness to the West increasing from $3.0 billion in 1975 to $3.2 billion in 1976. One factor to consider is debt service. Romania has a debt service approaching one-half of the value of hard-currency exports—or more than one-third of hard-currency earnings. Poland has a greater debt-service ratio than Romania but has greater hard-currency earnings, particularly from invisible earnings from Poles in the United States. Nevertheless, the Polish debt is large, and it has had to scale downward planned purchases from the West. The Polish economic plan for 1976-80, though calling for somewhat slower industrial growth, implies a continued hard-currency deficit and an increased debt burden.

Accurate financial data on East-West trade are often difficult to obtain. Western banks do not disclose the volume of their loans to the socialist countries. Western government agencies that insure credits of exporters do not reveal the amount of subsidies they give to promote trade. The socialist countries do not publish specific reserve, credit, or balance-of-payments statistics. However, calculations indicate that four major countries—France, Japan, the United States, and West Germany—have the bulk of the trade surplus with the socialist countries. West Germany is the largest holder of the surplus, with 40 percent of the total, followed by the United States with 25 percent. The debt of the socialist countries is held primarily by British banks, often operating in syndicates with U.S. banks. West German banks are also of importance, holding around 25 percent of the socialist debt. Most of the remainder of the debt is held by French, Italian, and Japanese financial institutions.

The socialist countries have a good record of debt repayment, and their debt problems are not as bad as many Western nations. The chances of default are low, because it is felt that the governments of the socialist countries can force out of their economies whatever is needed to meet financial obligations. However, the imbalance in East-West trade and the magnitude of the debt have resulted in a decline in the credit rating of some countries. Bulgaria, Poland, and Romania are no longer given the lowest interbank interest rates on their loans with Western financial institutions. Western banks can require the signing of detailed contracts that call for immediate repayment in the event of a default to any other lender. Western bankers have come to look at the projected future performance of socialist exports, and given the many impediments to greater trade, it would be unrealistic to assume they will vanish in the immediate future. Such influences as continued economic integration among the socialist countries can mean lower hard-currency export capacity and reduced gross foreign exchange receipts, resulting in lower borrowing capacity.

Experts have long held to the view that the trade gap between East and West can never be closed until the socialist countries can sell more manufactured goods of a better quality in Western markets. There continue to be problems in the marketing and the quality of goods for export as well as certain deficiencies in domestic production. To resolve these problems, socialist financial managers have had recourse to several solutions. They try to hedge against convertible-currency exchange movements by attempting to pay off debts in currencies that are expected to appreciate in value and slowing the rate of payment on loans in currencies that are expected to depreciate in value. To reduce the imbalance in trade, imports of nonessential Western goods have been reduced, while many large capital projects have been curtailed to conserve hard currency. The socialist countries have come to place more emphasis on various cooperation agreements that tend to circumvent the need to import and thus lose hard currency. To keep credit needs to a minimum the socialist countries have come to place greater emphasis on complex countertrade agreements, including barter arrangements. Coproduction agreements that minimize cash outlays and provide for a buy-back of output are strongly favored.

There are two factors that inhibit socialist exports to the West. First, internal domestic prices have virtually no relation to production costs and to demand factors that determine domestic prices in market-economy countries. Instead of reflecting scarcities or oversupplies, consumer demand or lack of it, or costs of labor, materials, and transport, prices are rigidly fixed and maintained by a central planning authority. A second factor involves foreign exchange rates. Socialist currencies are nonconvertible. Their exchange rates for Western currencies are arbitrarily fixed by their respective governments and are not in any way determined by the supply of, and demand for, a particular currency for trade, payment for services, and other transactions. Socialist prices are "disequilibria prices" in comparison with the way prices are determined in Western countries. This may hold down inflation, as it exists in Western countries, but it results in a completely unrealistic price structure as far as Western yardsticks are concerned. Then, too, the methods and factors used to determine costs and prices differ in varying degrees among the socialist countries.

Long-Term Business Agreements

Trade between East and West involves far more than a simple exchange of imports and exports between Western firms and foreign-trade organizations of the socialist countries. East-West commercial exchanges have increased in both volume and complexity. While the major portion of East-West trade continues to be individually negotiated export and import transactions, there is an ever-increasing volume of trade occurring under agreements that bind Western firms and socialist state enterprises and foreign-trade organizations into some form of cooperative business arrangement that goes beyond the sale of goods and services to each other. From simple exchange transactions, these arrangements have come to involve licensing, co-production, joint marketing, and other agreements that come under the category of industrial cooperation. Involved are relationships in which Western firms and their counterparts in the Eastern European countries engage in complementary or reciprocal matching operations in production, the development and exchange of technology, and marketing. In the socialist countries direct foreign investment by capitalist firms is generally prohibited, and the means of production are owned by the state. Industrial-cooperation agreements are a substitute means by which Western firms, with the approval of a socialist government, can penetrate socialist markets and earn a return on their investments.

U.S. multinational corporations are rather late partners in industrial-cooperation ventures with the socialist countries, and, as a result, European and Japanese firms have a substantial lead in developing commercial relations with Eastern Europe. However, the involvement between multinational corporations and the socialist countries is still in its infancy, and improved relations between the United States and Eastern Europe have opened up the possibility of sizable long-term business ventures on the part of U.S. corporations in this socialist sphere of influence. Nevertheless, a caveat is in order: The key to increased participation on the part of U.S. firms in the socialist economies lies in the continuation of reasonably good political relations between the United States and the Soviet Union. An increase in political hostility can exacerbate U.S. commercial relations with the Soviet Union and the countries of Eastern Europe that are within the Soviet orbit. By linking civil rights to MFN status for the Soviet Union, a limitation is placed on the terms and availability of credit for East-West trade. Furthermore, the Eastern European countries will remain heavily involved in the CMEA because their ability in the short or medium term to restructure their economies toward increased trade with the Western countries is limited.

SUMMARY

Détente between the United States and the Soviet Union was accompanied by a drastic increase in trade between the two countries and opened up the prospects for business participation on the part of U.S. corporations not only in the Soviet Union but in other Eastern European countries as well. These countries have come to share the capitalistic goals of economic growth and consumer abundance and have introduced certain capitalist principles such as a modified profit system and interplant competition. However, for the most part, there has been the need to increase productivity in order to maintain defense priorities and satisfy consumers' rising demand for a better material life. It is felt that a massive importation of Western technology and management skills to improve industrial production, along with the purchase of some consumer goods from the West, will go a long way to increase productivity and to satisfy consumer demand. To a major degree the opening up of the Soviet Union and its Eastern satellites to trade with Western countries is designed to obviate the need for continued economic reforms designed to provide greater individual incentives and more decentralization of production.

The pattern of economic relations between capitalist and socialist countries has undergone considerable change in recent years — from only limited commercial contact to a rather drastic increase in trade. There has also been an increase in various types of business arrangements between capitalist multinational corporations and socialist state enterprises and foreign-trade organizations. This arrangement may be of importance to both U.S. and Western European business firms. To the U.S. or West German business firms, Eastern Europe can constitute a potentially lucrative market for goods and services—a market that can be increased by the presence of the firm in some sort of business arrangement with a socialist state enterprise or foreign-trade organization. In fact, economic circumstances have favored the development of various forms of industrial-cooperation agreements, for a major obstacle to increased trade between Eastern and Western countries is the West's low demand for Eastern products. Without being able to export their products, the Eastern European countries are not in a position to earn the foreign exchange necessary to pay for exports from the West. A solution is cooperation agreements between Western and Eastern enterprises, involving arrangements ranging from the manufacture of semiconductors in Romania to the development of natural gas in Siberia.

NOTES

1. Although most of the Soviet Union is in Asia, the Western area, in which the seat of authority lies, is in Eastern Europe.

2. Henry Z. Horbaczewski, "Profitable Coexistence: The Legal Foundation for Joint Enterprises with U.S. Participation in Poland," Business Lawyer 31 (November 1975): 443.

3. Barnabas Buky, "Hungary on a Treadmill," Problems of Communism, September-October 1972, pp. 31-39.

4. U.S., Department of Commerce, Survey of International Economic Policy and Research, Trade of the United States with Communist Countries in Eastern Europe and Asia, Overseas Business Reports (Washington, D.C.: Government Printing Office, June 1977), p. 2.

5. Ibid., p. 5.

6. U.S., Department of Commerce, Bureau of East-West Trade, U.S.-U.S.S.R. Trade Trends (Washington, D.C.: Government Printing Office, June 1977), p. 9.

7. U.S., Department of Commerce, Bureau of East-West Trade, U.S.-Polish Trade Trends (Washington, D.C.: Government Printing Office, July 1977), p. 8.

8. The Export-Import Bank Amendment included a limit of $300 million on new loan commitments to the Soviet Union without further congressional approval. It also stipulated that no funds could be applied to energy production facilities without congressional approval.

9. U.S., Tariff Commission, United States-East European Trade: Consideration Involved in Granting Most Favored Nation Treatment to the Countries of Eastern Europe, prepared by Anton F. Malish (Staff Research Studies, no. 4), 1972, p. 18.

10. U.S., Department of Commerce, The United States Role in East-West Trade: Problems and Prospects (Washington, D.C.: Government Printing Office, August 1975), p. 35.

11. Agricultural export credits are supported by the Commodity Credit Corporation (CCC). Under the CCC export credit sales program, loans are not made directly to foreign governments. Instead, the CCC finances exports of eligible U.S. agricultural commodities by purchasing private U.S. exporters' accounts receivable. All transactions are ensured by irrevocable commercial letters of credit from acceptable banks.

2

INDUSTRIAL COOPERATION
BETWEEN EAST AND WEST:
BENEFITS AND CONSTRAINTS

It can be said that direct foreign investment by U.S. and other Western firms has a greater impact on balance of payments and world trade than simple direct exports and imports of goods and services.[1] There has been a shift from direct exports and imports to direct foreign investment, which can be explained by the fact that products traded in past times—food, cotton, coal, and steel—required no connection or communication between producer and consumer. They could be, and were, shipped and sold through intermediaries; the producer never saw the user. However, international trade has become far more sophisticated as products have become more complex. The marketing of these products requires a well-controlled sales organization, as well as instruction, repair, and service units. There is also need for control over the price of the final product. This means that the modern industrial corporation must have some influence and power over its own markets—over prices, costs, and means of consumer persuasion. This can best be achieved by direct foreign investments in countries where there are markets. In addition, where advanced technology is involved, foreign investments can realize economies of scale—the returns on one development cost are realized in several or numerous national markets.

The shift from exports and imports of goods and services to direct foreign investment has been expedited by a relatively new phenomenon, the modern multinational corporation. It is producing an organizational revolution as profound in its implications as the rise of the nation-state and the Industrial Revolution. These corporations now have the power to act as an agent of change on society, economies, and culture; yet they were formed and shaped by those very same forces and needs. The multinational corporation has emerged as the most sophisticated type of organization yet developed to integrate economic activity on an international basis. It transcends national boundaries and it produces more and more of the world's gross national product (GNP). Some of the current multinational corporations have sales volumes larger than the GNPs of many middle-sized European countries and sizably larger than the GNPs of typical underdeveloped African and Asian countries. But size is only one component of their power; they control the means of creating wealth and make decisions that have an economic impact on millions of people.

The multinational corporations have contributed to the internationalization of production, and in this process their investment decisions can be viewed in terms of world allocations of resources and maximizing world welfare. As mentioned above international production has surpassed foreign trade as the main vehicle for international relations in terms of size, rate of growth, and future potential. This calls traditional economic analysis into question. In foreign trade the conventional wisdom, as imparted by Adam Smith and David Ricardo, held to the principle of comparative advantage—that is, a situation where a nation's absolute cost advantage with respect to another nation in one particular commodity is relatively greater than its absolute cost advantage in any other commodity. From this theorem it was concluded that a nation should specialize in those things it does best, with a minimum of restrictions, and import those things that other nations produce more efficiently. What this meant was that commodities would flow back and forth between nations, but the factors of production would not. Capital movements, and hence international investments, were regarded as a temporary disturbance of foreign-trade equilibrium, which at times required government intervention in order to preserve a viable monetary system and a stable balance of payments.

The internationalization of production affects both the capitalist and socialist countries. Western firms are involved in the movement of productive resources, particularly capital, to the socialist countries. Conversely, socialist state trading monopolies have moved productive resources to the West. In commerce between the market economies of the West, there is a relatively free flow of investment capital and technology across national boundaries in the normal process of foreign investment. In the socialist countries, however, the means of production are owned by the state, and, although there are some exceptions in which minority interests can be owned by foreign firms, foreign direct investment is generally prohibited. To compensate for this fact agreements have developed between Western firms and socialist state enterprises that come under the category of industrial-cooperation arrangements. They provide Western firms with a substitute means by which to penetrate socialist markets and earn an additional return on their investments. They involve transactions in which Eastern and Western partners engage in reciprocally matching operations in production and distribution.

Industrial-cooperation arrangements between Western firms and state enterprises in the Soviet Union and Eastern Europe have expanded during the current decade and can be expected to continue to expand in the future, subject to the state of political tensions that exist between East and West. Thus, in the remainder of this chapter, the advantages and problems of industrial cooperation for both Western firms and socialist state enterprises will be discussed in some detail. In Chapter 3 various forms of industrial-cooperation agreements will also be discussed.

In the area of industrial cooperation U.S. firms have generally lagged well behind Western European competitors in their extent of involvement. Of 300 Hungarian industrial-cooperation agreements with the West, some 170 involve West German firms.[2] But U.S. firms enjoy some competitive advantages in industrial-cooperation arrangements, especially in licensing and coproduction, since U.S. technology is highly respected and recognized as the source of much of the commercial technology currently in use in Europe. Further, in turnkey projects, the United States is recognized as perhaps the only logical source of some of the large-scale industrial complexes sought by the Soviet Union and other Eastern socialist countries.

MOTIVES FOR INDUSTRIAL COOPERATION

Sorting out the motives underlying either individual or collective behavior is a very complex process not readily amenable to quantification or to generalization. Firms may be motivated by offensive or defensive strategies. Probably the most important motive is an obvious one—a search for new sources of profit. For a capitalist enterprise there may be the need to prevent market preemption by a competitor or to keep market outlets or sources of supply open. As foreign markets expand some economies of scale may be realized by producing abroad. Certain industries are by nature international, and their motives for investing abroad are readily apparent. The petroleum industry is an example. Its sources of raw materials are located abroad, and exploiting them requires establishing international production and marketing facilities. Another motive is that of diversifying product lines as a hedge against business recessions or strikes. A firm may also attempt to link its technological and managerial capacity to low-cost production inputs in other countries.

Attempts have been made to develop a theory of direct foreign investment—something that would explain the expansion of national firms into international ones. Several theories have been developed.

One theory suggests that firms with a monopolistic advantage expand into foreign markets to exploit their advantage abroad. Another theory holds that firms, particularly in oligopolistic industries, encounter limits to increasing the sales of their traditional product in the domestic market. To continue their growth, they must choose between expanding across a product boundary in the domestic market or expanding across a national boundary with their traditional product. The latter will be done if the economies of scale in domestic production are less than the cost of transportation to, and tariffs in, the foreign country. A third theory involves the interaction of oligopolistic firms,[3] and a fourth involves what is called the "product life cycle" model, which traces the maturation of a product from its development and domestic sale to its export and, finally, to its production by a subsidiary abroad.[4] These last two theories are explained below.

Oligopolistic Factors

Oligopoly refers to a market situation in which there are a few sellers of a differentiated product. Many U.S. and Western European industries conform to the pattern of oligopoly. The steel, automobile, and cigarette industries are examples. In fact, oligopoly seems to be characteristic of industries where modern methods of production are applicable. The pattern for oligopolistic industries is for there to be a few giant firms that account for one-half or more of total industry output, followed by smaller firms that produce the rest. For example, General Motors and Ford account for at least two-thirds of automobile sales by U.S. car manufacturers. Typical of most oligopolistic industries is mass merchandising, which involves distinguishing a firm's product from those of its competitors by means of branding and trademarks and creating a preference for the brand by means of advertising. However, some industries approach a situation called pure oligopoly. Here the firms in the industry produce virtually identical products. Buyers have little cause for preferring the product of one firm to that of another on any basis except price. Examples of industries that approach being pure oligopolies are the aluminum, cement, and steel industries.

Oligopolistic industries have several important characteristics. First, no one firm can profit by adhering to price competition. For example, if a firm raises its price and others do not follow suit, it is usually out of luck in terms of sales. Conversely, if the same firm lowers its price and the others do not follow, all the firms that do not lower their prices could lose business. Consequently, all firms are almost certain to follow with lower prices, so that they all end up with the same share of the market, though selling at a lower price. Second, in the absence of price competition, firms, tacitly or otherwise, reach some sort of agreement as to what a set price should be. There may be a leader, usually the largest firm in the industry, that sets the price, and other firms merely follow the leader. What competition there is takes the form of product differentiation.

Most U.S. and Western European direct investment in other countries is concentrated within a few industries, and the market structure of these industries is generally dominated by a few firms. Thus, oligopolistic conditions are present. One essential characteristic of oligopolistic industries is the interdependence of firms in making decisions. In contemplating a new product, a price change, or an investment, each firm must speculate on the reactions of other firms in the industry. Investment moves by one firm are followed with similar moves by other leading firms in the industry. No follower wants to run the risk of a rival firm gaining an advantage from a profitable foreign investment that could be used against it later in the domestic market. In the case of Eastern Europe there is always the possibility that Western European enterprises can capture this market, thus threatening the world competitive position of U.S. and Japanese enterprises. The firms pursue a follow-the-leader or defensive strategy.

The Product Life Cycle Model

The product life cycle model also attempts to explain why firms invest abroad. According to this theory, a product goes through several stages of development. The first stage is the creation of the product, and the second stage is its introduction into the domestic market. The next stage is the export of the product. As the product matures it becomes more standardized, and the possibility of its being imitated and produced overseas by a foreign firm increases. If the product has a high income elasticity of demand, or if it is a satisfactory substitute for high-cost labor, the demand for it, particularly in the more advanced countries, may grow rapidly. Then the firm has to make a decision as to whether to invest in a foreign subsidiary. As long as the marginal production cost of the product plus the cost to transport it abroad is lower than the average cost of having a subsidiary produce it in the export market, the firm will probably avoid investment in a subsidiary. However, if the product begins to be produced by foreign manufacturers, the firm is likely to set up a foreign subsidiary in order to maintain its market share abroad and to recapture the remaining rent from the product's development. The local market will then be filled by production units from the subsidiary.

Eventually, the subsidiary—located, say, in France—may serve third-country markets so as to exploit economies of scale. If cost differences are large enough to offset transportation costs, then the subsidiary may even export back to the United States. It may be added that, once one firm undertakes an investment in a foreign country, competing firms may be galvanized into action in order to maintain the status quo. Their share of the market, viewed in global terms, may be threatened. And their ability to estimate the production cost of their competitor, operating in a foreign market area, is impaired by their inability to assess foreign conditions. Any uncertainty can be reduced by imitating the original investing company and investing in the same geographic area. In the final stages of the product life cycle, new competitors arise to challenge the position of the original firms. Saturation of existing markets appears imminent, ultimately, and it becomes necessary to look for new markets.

Although investment decisions are usually the result of a complex amalgam of factors, there is some evidence to support both the oligopolistic and product life cycle theories. Modern multinational corporations, regardless of the country of origin, usually represent industries that are oligopolistic in nature. Defensive considerations are often responsible for investing in another country. Once one firm makes a move, others follow suit, and the structure of the oligopoly remains undisturbed. If no move is made by the other firms, the balance of power within the oligopoly may well shift to the firm that did make a move. A study of 37 West German firms operating in Eastern Europe, which was conducted by the Institut für Aussenhandel und Überseewirtschaft der Universität Hamburg, indicates that a prime motive for the involvement of these firms in Eastern Europe was to extend the sales life of products already on the decline in other markets.[5] Another motive was to gain marketing advantages over other Western competitors.

Benefits of Industrial Cooperation
to Western Enterprises

Certain benefits can be derived by Western firms from industrial-cooperation agreements with Eastern European foreign-trade organizations and state enterprises. These benefits can be cataloged under the following topics: access to markets, political and social stability, stable labor conditions, comprehensive education, lower operating costs, and new technology. The two most important benefits appear to be access to markets and lower operating costs.

Access to Markets

Western firms have recognized the fact that the socialist countries represent one of the largest potential markets in the world, with the added bonus of having stable business conditions, at least in comparison with Africa, Asia, and Latin America. As a group the Eastern European countries are experiencing economic growth and development superior to, or on a par with, other regions of the world. More important, economic growth and reforms in these nations have created the formation of a built-in demand for technology and marketing know-how possessed by U.S. and other Western firms. Many Western firms, through aggressive leadership, have had the opportunity to shape this new market development and reap the benefits of their initiative. Special relations among the socialist economies often provide a relatively simple vehicle for Western firms to penetrate into other socialist markets, once operations are established in one country. This, in itself, provides an important benefit to Western firms. Numerous bilateral trade and cooperation agreements exist between the socialist nations and the developing countries of the Third World. The trade restrictions of the developing countries can be circumvented through business operations conducted in the socialist nations.

Political and Social Stability

Insecurity of commercial operations in many parts of the world, resulting from unstable political and social factors (Italy is a case in point), has increased the interest of Western firms in industrial-cooperation arrangements with the socialist countries. Relatively stable governments with low-profile foreign policies are a prime desideratum of international business. In addition, the socialist countries have domestic stability, if not tranquillity, and a well-developed infrastructure. This is often more favorable to Western business than the uncertain political and social environment in the developing countries of the Third World. There is, at least for the present, greater acceptance of U.S. and Western business operations in the socialist countries, and socialist foreign-trade organizations and state enterprises have much to offer because of state emphasis on economic development. There are strong inducements for industrial cooperation, which have been accomplished through the growth of mutual commercial interests and increased economic convergence between East and West.

Stable Labor Conditions

Labor unions, which present adversary problems to business in most Western countries, do not create similar problems in the socialist countries. Socialist labor unions are an appendage of the state and, as such, do not engage in strikes, shutdowns, or other tactics against management. All labor relations are ironed out by the state and stipulated when an agreement is reached with a Western firm. Wages are set by the state in conformance with the rubric of the national economic plan. Although it was originally intended that important managerial decisions would be made by a troika of management, labor, and party representatives, the role of the union has declined in importance as the drive for industrial efficiency has strengthened managerial authority. Thus, the Eastern European countries offer to Western business firms a relatively low-paid, pliable labor force, which includes skilled technical personnel, and a degree of industrial concentration in many industries that allows for very large-scale operations.

Comprehensive Education

The socialist countries have a very comprehensive system of education, which contributes to the skills of the labor force. In many countries, but in particular the developing nations, the labor force is usually unskilled, untrained, and often illiterate. There is an absence of trained workers of all types. These factors place the burden of training on foreign firms, if they plan to utilize the local labor force. Social expenditures, including those on education, have always had a high priority in the socialist countries, with the result that there are numerous universities and technical schools. These schools can provide Western firms operating in Eastern Europe with a capable and well-educated pool of employees and an opportunity to take advantage of improved technology and innovation.

Lower Operating Costs

The socialist countries are still relatively isolated from economic pressures originating in the West by an extensive system of exchange and trade barriers. Furthermore, they continue an economic and political policy of controlling production and prices and setting artificial price relationships. Although it is difficult to establish costs of production for socialist state enterprises because different criteria for price setting are used for different categories of products, it is generally agreed that the cost of operation in the socialist countries is lower than in the Western countries. This is especially true of labor costs, since wages are changed as deemed necessary to effect government policies and achieve particular production ends. U.S. and other Western firms can benefit from lower production costs by contracting with socialist enterprises to manufacture not only finished goods but parts and subassemblies for distribution to their sub-

sidiaries in high-wage areas. Because of the proximity of the socialist countries to Western developed markets, U.S. and other firms
can form business relations with socialist state enterprises and foreign-trade organizations to have a source of better quality and greater
productivity than is available from operating in developing countries.

New Technology

The transfer of technology is not limited to Western firms; to
the contrary, it is a two-way phenomenon. There is an increasing
similarity in the industrial structures of East and West. Available
statistics point to growing international production specialization
within both Eastern and Western industrial nations. One measure of
the two-way transfer of technology involves the granting of patent
rights by the Eastern European countries, including the Soviet Union,
to the Western nations and the number of patent rights granted by the
Western nations to the East. In 1965 the West granted 2,065 patent
rights to the East, while the East granted 676 patent rights to the
West.[6] In 1973 the West granted 5,663 patent rights to the East, but
the East granted 5,965 patent rights to the West. One example of
technology transfer involved the Hungarian-designed compact refuse
burner, which can be operated with natural gas, gas oil, or light fuel
oil.[7] Patent rights to manufacture this product have been granted to
firms in France, Italy, and West Germany.

Benefits of Industrial Cooperation
to Socialist Enterprises

The benefits of industrial cooperation to socialist enterprises
are somewhat similar to those that accrue to capitalist enterprises.
There is access to Western technology and expertise in marketing,
an area in which socialist enterprises are weak. Another important
benefit is access to Western capital markets through association with
a large Western enterprise. There is a close relationship between
Western banks, which operate on a global basis, and the capitalist
multinational corporations. Contracts with the latter provide access
to the major Western banks. Industrial cooperation also affords the
socialist enterprises opportunities to increase exports to the West,
thus improving earnings of hard currency needed to purchase imports
from the West.

Advanced Technology

The most important motive for socialist industrial cooperation
with Western firms has been the need to acquire advanced technology,

with the increase in efficiency and productivity that such technology provides. The current strategy of socialist state enterprises is based on intensive growth, which is built upon the availability of advanced technology and know-how. One economic justification advanced in support of the large Western multinationals is their alleged superiority in science and management technology. Therefore, through their vast research and development resources and worldwide operations, large Western firms can provide not only the necessary technology but also its immediate application. The effects of closer socialist economic ties with the West include the development and manufacture of new products and the application of new industrial processes. Economic reforms in the socialist countries have been designed to reduce economic problems and to create conditions more suitable for efficient industrial operations. This has helped to create an environment in which, at least for the present, specialization and economies of scale can take place.

Sources of Capital

The greatest restraining factor in Western business arrangements with socialist state enterprises and foreign-trade organizations is their lack of hard currency. Long-term contractual arrangements with Western firms can be used to help alleviate this problem. Direct private investment by capitalist enterprises is limited to only a few of the Eastern European countries, but through ties with Western firms, socialist state enterprises and foreign-trade organizations have been able to obtain Western hard currency. Under certain contractual arrangements, a state enterprise or foreign-trade organization may secure the necessary currency directly from the assets of a Western firm, or, because of its high credit rating, the firm may raise needed capital in Western financial markets for the benefit of the state-enterprise partner. A Western firm can also provide supplier credit to the state enterprise in the form of materials or equipment. Hard-currency requirements can be reduced through contributions of technology or raw materials, while payments can often be made in the form of manufactured products.

Political Independence of Western Multinationals

Political leaders and plant managers in the socialist countries have recognized that the typical large U.S. or West German multinational firm has developed into an economic institution that operates with a considerable degree of independence from both home and host nations.[8] Although these firms have the potential to change international relations, they are to a large degree divorced from the political influence of government. The typical large U.S. or German firm does not have an ingrained ideological drive but is motivated, rather, by the pragmatic concept of economic gain. A case in point is Occidental Petroleum, which had been active in commercial operations with the Soviet Union long before détente. The socialist enterprises are able to develop closer economic ties with the large capitalist firms without having to accept the political influence of the governments they nominally represent. Thus, the socialist countries, through the creation of transideological arrangements with Western firms, can exert tight control over the commercial activities of their state enterprises to protect their national economic interests.

Access to Markets

The distribution of goods is one area in which the socialist countries are inadequate. Industrial cooperation with Western firms can provide socialist foreign-trade organizations with long-term contracts that provide a means of egress into Western markets. Market access on a large scale permits foreign-trade organizations and state enterprises to have a greater share of stability in export operations, which assists in the implementation of their own economic and social growth strategy. Entries into new markets can provide the conditions necessary for economies of scale and specialization in production to take place. One of the greatest competitive disadvantages that continues to plague socialist foreign-trade organizations in world markets is their lack of sufficient entrepreneurial and managerial talent. The worldwide marketing operations and the distribution expertise of Western firms can help socialist foreign-trade organizations to reduce the risks and high costs of international operations. In addition, managers of state enterprises can gain valuable experience and marketing skills by working in conjunction with Western firms.

New Sources of Supply

Industrial-cooperation agreements with Western firms can provide foreign-trade organizations and state enterprises with additional deliveries of raw materials, parts, or even finished goods from worldwide sources of supply. This enables state–enterprise managers to avoid production problems caused by distribution inefficiencies, limitations in the choice of suppliers, or a generally poor performance by subcontracting state enterprises. A major problem in production in the socialist countries is a breakdown in distribution among state enterprises. Often production facilities lie idle because suppliers have failed to provide the requisite raw materials or parts on time. While the Soviet Union supplies a large part of Eastern European imports of plants and equipment for mining, metallurgy, transport, agriculture, and public utlities, Soviet industry has done little, if anything, to meet the needs of the rapidly growing chemical industry in Eastern Europe or of the revived and expanding light and food industries. To develop these sectors in particular, the Eastern European countries have had to turn to the West for sources of capital equipment, parts, and components.

A high regard for Western technology is well documented in Soviet and Eastern European sources. In official negotiations between Eastern and Western governments and in private business agreements with Western enterprises, Eastern officials have shown the most interest in those areas in which the West appears to have a legitimate claim to world technological leadership. One such area is large-scale petroleum and natural gas extraction, transmission, and distribution systems, including those designed to help solve specific permafrost problems. An example involves the formation of ventures between U.S. firms and the Soviet Union to develop the natural gas resources of Siberia. Another area is the use of machinery, equipment, and know-how needed to modernize the production of basic industries, such as automobiles and chemicals. Increasing concern for consumer welfare and the promotion of tourism to attract hard currency have also led to socialist imports of technology ranging from soft drinks to motels and hotels.[9] Each of these technological areas requires large-scale financing, consortium operations, and marketing systems, all of which can be provided by Western business firms.

RESTRAINTS ON INDUSTRIAL COOPERATION

There are restraining factors that need to be considered in examining the potential for a continuation of industrial-cooperation agreements between capitalist and socialist governments. Suspicion on both sides has often made cooperation difficult. In addition, there are many legislative and bureaucratic restrictions that can slow or prevent commercial relations from taking place. Slow and complex decision making by bureaucrats is not conducive to long-term business relations between socialist state enterprises and Western multinational corporations under rapidly changing world economic conditions. Many Western firms have not been aware of business opportunities in Eastern Europe because of the lack of information provided by their governments. Uncertainty about the future of political relations between East and West may make many Western firms hesitant to invest capital resources and to develop commercial relations with the Eastern European countries. Long-term examples of profitable business ventures in Eastern Europe will have a decidedly salutary effect on increasing the volume of business between Western firms and socialist state enterprises and foreign-trade organizations.

Capitalist Restraints

On the capitalist side the international political and economic policy of the United States has been the most important influence on commercial policy between East and West. This means that much of the success for a favorable continuation of East-West commercial relations depends upon the fragile rubric of détente between the United States and the Soviet Union. There has been a tendency on the part of the U.S. government to minimize economic considerations and view commercial relations with the Soviet Union and Eastern Europe primarily within the political context of détente. The Soviets, too, tie economic relations to political developments. But while the Soviets have held to the idea that U.S. willingness to improve relations in the economic sphere is a measure of the United States' good faith and must therefore precede political and military détente, the U.S. government has reversed this linkage, arguing that greater economic exchange can only follow in the wake of a Soviet show of goodwill on the international and political fronts. Increased commercial relations is the bait that is supposed to lead the Soviets toward political and military accommodations with the United States.

Because many industrial cooperation agreements involve the sale of factories, on-site participation by U.S. companies, and the sale of finished products back to the United States as the method of payment, the transactions have assumed many of the characteristics of U.S. investment in other parts of the world. This extension of commercial relationships beyond simple export and import transactions raises a series of difficult questions for the United States in the areas of national security and international competition. During the cold war, a central objective of U.S. economic policy was to hinder the economic growth of the Soviet Union and to block any Soviet access to Western technology with potential military applicability. However, while the Soviet Union is still regarded as the single most serious military threat to U.S. security, such considerations have to be reconciled with a policy of actively promoting greater East-West trade and investment. The resultant increase in the volume of trade and the new complexity of economic ties with the socialist countries have raised difficult issues about the nature of commercial relations between free market economies and state trading monopolies, which were considered of little relevance in the past.

There also continue to be numerous regulatory factors that limit industrial cooperation between East and West. Many controls are maintained by the capitalist nations for the ostensible purpose of promoting foreign policy objectives, ensuring national security, or preventing the export of strategic raw materials. An absence of the most-favored nation (MFN) clause provides an obstacle to U.S. dealings with some socialist countries. Public pressure, particularly in the United States, can prevent certain transactions between U.S. and socialist firms from occurring. Lobbyists can effectively block liberalization of regulatory restrictions and are in a position to link questions of internal national policy to industrial cooperation with the socialist countries. Ideological differences can cause emotional shifts in public opinion based on the contention that expansion of industrial cooperation between the United States and Eastern Europe will serve to strengthen the socialist bloc nations in relation to the capitalist nations. There is the fear that the United States may provide technical know-how to socialist countries that will use it to provide competition to the detriment of U.S. business interests. This can occur because true costs can be ignored and a product can be sold abroad below cost.

Socialist Restraints

The strongest restraining influence that bears directly on East-West industrial cooperation is the indebtedness of Eastern Europe to the West. This indebtedness stems from an extremely unfavorable balance of trade between East and West, with Eastern imports from the West far exceeding exports to the West. This one-sided relationship is exacerbated by the fact that around 80 percent of Western exports to Eastern Europe consist of manufactured goods, with exports of machinery and equipment accounting for one-half of the total. Conversely, exports from East to West consist primarily of agricultural products, raw materials, and fuels, although there is some export of manufactured goods. To some degree the structure of East-West trade very closely resembles the traditional pattern of trade between developed and developing regions. This presents a dilemma for the Eastern European countries. There is the need for Western equipment, plants, and technology, but the capacity for importing from the West is ultimately determined by an ability to sell products and obtain hard currency. But import demand for Eastern products in the West is growing relatively slowly, and many products are subject to restrictive quotas in some Western countries and the lack of MFN status in the United States.

A second restraining factor that can impinge upon East-West industrial cooperation is the economic and political policy generated on a regional basis by the Council for Mutual Economic Assistance (CMEA) and the Warsaw Treaty Organization. Although both of these organizations are dominated by the Soviet Union, there are conflicting attitudes within the socialist countries with respect to industrial cooperation with the West. Economic and political constraints narrow the margin of action of most members of the CMEA. The goals and objectives of the member countries of the CMEA are subject to change as far as any institutionalized relationship between East and West is concerned. Although the Soviet Union has taken steps to lower commercial barriers between the CMEA and the capitalist countries in favor of a partial, although fragile, rapprochement with the highly industrialized Western nations and their institutions and organizations, changes in political attitudes toward the West can occur almost overnight. Then, too, such countries as Poland, Romania, and Hungary have attempted to expand their economic and political leverage through a greater opening to the West to limit the extent of Soviet influence and to gain economic benefits. Their efforts to achieve some independence may well conflict with Soviet self-interest.

The CMEA countries bring different interests to industrial negotiations with the West. There are sharp differences in the concerns of the Soviet Union and the smaller countries of the CMEA. The Soviet Union is an enormous country with an abundance of natural resources, and it can be expected to push hardest on interests that follow naturally from its comparative advantage. The Soviets would show an interest in enormous projects on Soviet soil where Western money and machinery exploit primary product and fuel resources now, with the resulting products shipped to the West later. However, unlike the Soviet Union, the other CMEA countries do not have a comparative advantage in natural resources such as fuels; instead, they have to rely for a substantial portion of their foreign-exchange earnings in the West on agricultural and food exports. But these exports run into agricultural import restrictions in Western Europe. Thus, in the absence of natural resources and with restrictions placed on imports of food products, there is some lack of a commonality of interest between most CMEA countries and Western Europe.

This does not rule out industrial cooperation, since other factors do exist to favor arrangements, at least in the area of manufactured goods. The burgeoning industrial-cooperation agreements between East and West have demonstrated that countries such as Hungary and Poland have a relative abundance of cheap labor, which can best be exploited in a number of small cooperation agreements between Western and Eastern enterprises. These agreements are less spectacular than the much larger agreements between consortia of Western firms and the Soviet Union in which billions of dollars are involved, but they can be profitable to all who are involved. The smaller CMEA countries are in a position to improve their manufacturing exports, at least to Western Europe, which has been a major market area. Imports of manufacturing are much more important than from the Soviet Union, and the share has increased substantially from 38 percent in 1965 to 55 percent in 1975. However, the potential for export of manufactured goods is restrained not only by Western trade barriers but also by an inferior product quality relative to Western products, as well as by the lack of sophistication of Eastern managerial and marketing practices.

Finally, it is necessary to take the economic plans of the socialist countries into consideration. The current five-year plans of the Eastern European countries call for economic retrenchment. Through expanded East-West economic relations, the Eastern European countries had hoped to import Western technology to expand output, stimulate technological progress, increase exports, and satisfy demands of their populations. However, these hopes are constrained by an inability to earn hard-currency exports fast enough. Initially, the gap was covered by Western credits, but outstanding indebtedness is now large—particularly for Poland but also for other Eastern countries—and serving the debt absorbs a large and rising portion of export earnings. Imports from the West are to be reduced in the current five-year plans, and industrial-cooperation agreements with Western firms are to be considered only within a framework that involves the earning of hard currency. The central authorities are likely to retain close control over hard-currency exports and imports, as well as negotiations with foreign banks for credits and with foreign firms for industrial-cooperation ventures.

SUMMARY

Improved trade between East and West has created opportunities for various types of business ventures. Consequently, an increasing number of Western firms have become active in developing business arrangements with the Soviet Union and the Eastern European bloc countries. There are benefits to both East and West from these arrangements. For the East such arrangements mean better access to Western technology and related production and management know-how, and they help attract Western capital. The use of a Western partner to assist in the production and marketing of products destined for Western markets improves the hard-currency-earnings position of the Eastern partner. Benefits to capitalist firms include access to new markets and new technology, lower production costs, and a stable political and economic environment in which to operate. On balance large U.S. and Western firms may well be a key factor in an evolution toward equilibrium between the capitalist and socialist systems, which is a result of efforts to create conditions for the more effective use of resources.

There are also problems involved in East-West industrial cooperation. For one thing ideological differences exist between the capitalist and socialist nations. A lack of hard currency on the part

of socialist enterprises and foreign-trade organizations also presents a problem. Because many industrial-cooperation agreements between the United States and the Soviet Union and Eastern Europe involve the sale of factories, on-site participation by U.S. companies, and the sale of finished products back to the United States as the method of payment, transactions can assume many of the characteristics of U.S. investment in other parts of the world. This extension of the commercial relationship beyond simple export and import transactions raises a series of difficult questions for the United States in the areas of national security and international competition. Finally, the new complexity of economic ties with the socialist countries has raised difficult issues about the nature of commercial relations between free market economies and state trading monopolies.

NOTES

1. U.S., Congress, Senate, Committee on Foreign Relations, Multinational Corporations and United States Foreign Policy: Hearing before the Subcommittee on Multinational Corporations, 93rd Cong., 2d sess., 1974, pp. 1-15.

2. Hungary, Ministry of Foreign Trade, Hungarian Economic Relations and Cooperative Ventures, prepared by Tibor Antalpeter (Budapest, Ministry of Foreign Trade, November 1977), p. 2.

3. Charles P. Kindleberger, American Business Abroad: Six Lectures on Direct Investment (New Haven, Conn.: Yale University Press, 1969), pp. 1-18.

4. Raymond Vernon, "International Investment and International Trade in the Product Life Cycle," Quarterly Journal of Economics 80 (1966): 190-207.

5. Institut für Aussenhandel und Überseewirtschaft der Universität Hamburg, Erfarungen aus der Ost-West-Kooperation (Hamburg: Verlag Weltarchir, 1976).

6. U.S., Congress, Joint Economic Committee, Technology, Economic Growth, and International Competitiveness: Report Prepared for Subcommittee on Economic Growth, 94th Cong., 1st sess., 1975.

7. Hungarian Chamber of Commerce, Hungarian Foreign Trade, Budapest, February 1978, p. 2.

8. U.S., Congress, Senate, Committee on Finance, Implications of Multinational Firms for World Trade and Investment and for U.S. Trade and Labor: Report to the Subcommittee on International Trade, 93rd Cong., 1st sess., 1973, pp. 80-83.

9. Edwin M. Snell, "East European Economics between the Soviets and the Capitalists," published in Joint Economic Committee, East European Economics Post-Helsinki: A Compendium of Papers (Washington, D.C.: U.S. Government Printing Office, 1977), p. 52.

3
FORMS OF
INDUSTRIAL COOPERATION

The development of trade between East and West has come to involve more than simple export and import transactions between capitalist firms and socialist foreign-trade organizations. There has been an increased volume of trade under agreements that bind both capitalist firms and socialist foreign-trade organizations into longer-term contractual relationships that come under the category of industrial cooperation. These relationships enable the capitalist and socialist countries to bridge the differences between their economic systems. In commerce between market economies there is a relatively free flow of investment capital and technology across national borders in the normal process of investment. In the socialist countries, however, the means of production are owned by the state, and although there are some exceptions in which minority interests can be generally owned by foreign parties, foreign investment is generally prohibited. Cooperative relationships are, therefore, to some degree a substitute means by which Western firms can penetrate socialist markets and earn an additional return on their investments in the research and development of the technology involved.

In this chapter various forms of industrial cooperation ranging from licensing agreements to turnkey plants will be discussed. U.S. corporations are relatively new at participating in East-West cooperation, but they have come on strong during this decade. But much of this growth has been made possible by Eastern European borrowing from Western governments, with the result that net indebtedness to the West has increased rather precipitously. The balance-of-payments problems of most of the Eastern European countries have been further exacerbated by a rise in the world prices of oil and other raw materials and by harvest failures, which have necessitated an increase in imports of agricultural products. Thus, in order to ameliorate pressure on hard-currency reserves, the Eastern European countries have made recourse to countertrade—a contractual obligation to purchase Eastern goods related to the Western sales of goods and services. It has become of increased importance in the long-run planning of the Eastern European countries and a factor that U.S. firms will have to consider if they wish to continue increased expansion into Eastern markets.

Now that diplomatic relations have been formalized with China, a new area of trade opportunity has opened up for U.S. business firms. Since its break with the Soviet Union, with which it had contracted a substantial debt, China's policy toward foreign involvement has been cautious. Nevertheless, China's contacts with the West can be expected to increase. Therefore, the discussion of industrial cooperation and countertrade is just as relevant to China as it is to Eastern Europe. China, like the Eastern European countries, must first overcome organizational and other deficiencies before its industries can be fully competitive in world markets. But China is aware of that fact and will look to Western firms to provide needed expertise.

INDUSTRIAL COOPERATION

There is no set definition of industrial cooperation. In general, it can be defined as a set of exchange relationships involving production and distribution at various levels of capitalist and socialist enterprises.[1] Usually there is some sort of a pooling arrangement in which the Eastern and Western partners provide assets and coordinate their use toward the attainment of a particular objective. There is a direct relation with the process of production, and, as opposed to trade, there is not a once-for-all transaction but an arrangement that lasts over a period of years and requires a continuing commitment from the partners involved. Industrial cooperation also involves the preservation of each partner's property rights—an important point because of the contrasting social structures and different systems of property relations existing in the capitalist and socialist countries. There are no formal equity links between the capitalist and socialist partners, except in joint ventures between the partners, based on joint-equity participation, profit and risk sharing, and joint management. These ventures are also limited to those socialist countries that permit them. Finally, industrial cooperation is characterized by a diversity of forms and a wide range of activities and levels of participation of capitalist and socialist industries.

On a legal basis industrial cooperation can be divided into two categories—joint-equity ventures and industrial-cooperation agreements. The former is not commonly used in business arrangements with the socialist countries, with the exception of Yugoslavia, a country that is not tied to the Eastern bloc either politically or socially and that has an atypically decentralized domestic economy. It is permitted, with some restraints, in Hungary, Poland, and Romania. The joint-equity-venture arrangement involves a property relationship based on equity ownership and shared property rights. There is the right to share profits, the distribution of assets, and participation in management. Ownership provides security for the invested capital and creates a basis for the rights of management. In comparison with industrial-cooperation agreements, joint ventures require a larger investment of resources, but there is more security provided against changes in the economic and political climate of the Eastern country.

Joint-equity ventures present a wide variety of commercial complexities created by the fact that there is the joining of a private, market-oriented enterprise and a state-owned and -operated enterprise. A U.S. firm entering into a joint-venture agreement with a socialist firm must be aware of the legal aspects of the agreement. For example, under Polish and Romanian laws, joint ventures enjoy the status of corporate legal entities and, as such, can sue and be sued; they operate under local commercial laws and are responsible for their own actions to the state. They are subject not only to the specific legislation affecting joint ventures but to all other laws as well. Polish and Romanian laws place restrictions on the transfer of ownership shares in a limited liability association, but even shares of joint-stock companies are difficult to dispose of. Both U.S.-Polish and U.S.-Romanian enterprises must go through an elaborate approval procedure before entering into a joint-equity agreement. The agreement must usually satisfy some need on the part of the socialist country, such as the development of projects for the manufacturing of goods that fulfill home-market requirements.

Industrial-cooperation agreements, on the other hand, do not involve equity participation on the part of the parties involved. There is no link of shared property rights, and there is minimal participation in terms of direct investment in the home country of one partner by the other. A smaller investment is needed, and since the partners share production functions, neither has to relinquish the means of production used in its part of the process. There is no requirement of prepaid capital, thus providing more flexibility in the commitment of resources. Unlike the joint-equity venture, industrial-cooperation agreements are subject to international law as opposed to the laws of the country in which the joint venture operates. The Code of Private International Law permits parties in an industrial-cooperation agreement to subject their contract to the law of any country that has a connection with the transaction, except as to immovables.[2] There are fewer problems in the transfer of property rights because there is no domestic market for the shares of a joint-equity venture, and the circumstances that could make the owner desirous to sell would probably make other foreign investors less than anxious to buy.

It is necessary to mention that industrial cooperation involves basic differences in the economic systems of capitalism and socialism. In the capitalist countries decisions to engage in industrial-cooperation agreements are made by private enterprises. In the socialist countries decisions to participate in industrial cooperation are made by state foreign-trade organizations within the rubric of the national economic plan. The agreements are an integral part of plans for foreign trade, investment, and production. The plans are subject to change, depending on the economic requirements of the time. Currently, the Eastern European countries have currency and credit problems—a shortage of hard currency and an overextension of credit—that impinge upon the expansion of industrial-cooperation agreements. But the main criterion is that industrial cooperation must be consistent with the goals and priorities of the national economic plan. An industrial-cooperation agreement that leads to an increase in productivity of socialist agriculture is regarded as more important than one that increases the number of color television sets for socialist viewers.

Types of Industrial Cooperation

Regardless of the definition of industrial cooperation, there are a number of different types of contractual arrangements that are reached between Western business firms and socialist state enterprises and foreign-trade organizations. These arrangements vary among the socialist countries, with Hungary, Poland, and Romania being the most liberal in terms of the variety permitted. During the period 1972-76, Hungary was involved in the signing of 170 cooperative agreements with firms from West Germany, Italy, France, the United States, and the United Kingdom. Romania sanctions direct investment by Western firms within its territory, provided that there is a joint-equity venture in which the government is the major shareholder. Paradoxically, the German Democratic Republic, the most industrially advanced of all the Eastern socialist countries, has the lowest degree of cooperative involvement with the West. In part this may be attributed to the fact that it remained diplomatically isolated from many Western countries. Recent changes in its political parameters, accompanied by such cogent economic factors as a lack of natural resources, have caused the German Democratic Republic to adopt a more positive attitude toward economic cooperation with the West.

There is a wide variety of industrial-cooperation arrangements ranging from licensing of patents and production know-how to contractual agreements for production on a continuing basis. There can be a package arrangement involving various types of industrial cooperation. A Western firm can provide a turnkey plant and the equipment and engage in joint international marketing. Because of their size and resources, Western multinationals are ideally suited to participate in these arrangements. In the initial stages of industrial cooperation with the Soviet Union and the Eastern European countries, it has been the large Western multinationals that have made the ventures and been willing to take the risks. To a considerable degree they have the resources, capital, and initiative to take advantage of business opportunities in the East. However, industrial-cooperation agreements are not the sole preserve of Western multinationals; consortia of smaller Western firms have been successful in developing agreements with the East.

Joint-Production Agreements

A common form of industrial cooperation is the coproduction agreement. It involves the production of a product that may be sold in Eastern Europe or in a Western market. A Western firm usually supplies the production technology and an Eastern state enterprise actually does the manufacturing. One example involves the French industrial firm, Berliet, a subsidiary of Regie-Renault, which has been manufacturing trucks and buses in Poland for ten years.[3] A new factory was built by the French in Warsaw to manufacture Jelez-Berliet buses, which are sold in Eastern and Western Europe and in Africa. Machine tools and equipment for the buses are made in Poland with the aid of French technical specialists. The Polish counterpart agency, Pol-Mot (transport) Foreign Trade Organization, is responsible for the provision of labor, raw materials, and certain industrial equipment and also for the export of the buses to Eastern Europe. Renault produces a wide range of buses and trucks in Western Europe and, through Berliet, sells around 40,000 trucks and buses annually in Poland, Hungary, and other Eastern bloc countries. Renault is interested in future joint-production operations with Poland, including the development of new lines of buses and trucks.

A proposed joint-production agreement between General Motors (GM) and Pol-Mot originated in 1975 with plans to build a new type of van in an expanded truck plant in Lublin, Poland. One aspect of the proposed joint-production agreement was that the vehicles were to be of an original design to meet Polish specificiations and not a modification or adaptation of an existing GM truck model. The British subsidiary of GM, Vauxhall, designed the new van. Poland would have exclusive marketing rights within the socialist countries, while GM would sell the vans in Western Europe. Much of the equipment required to expand and modernize the Lublin plant would be shipped from the United States. The engines for the plant would be supplied by Vauxhall. The estimated initial costs for plant modernization plus the engineering for the van total $600 million, with an initial commitment of $300 million from the U.S. side, supported by Export-Import Bank (Eximbank) credits for $165 million, and $105 million in credits supplied by a commercial bank consortium led by Morgan Guaranty. Production of vans at the Pol-Mot plant, if and when the venture is formally consummated, would reach 100,000 annually. [4]

There are other variants of product agreements. In contrast to the coproduction agreement, in which each partner may produce and sell the same end product, there can be product-specialization agreements in which there is vertical integration of the East and West partners. A Western firm could concentrate on a series of diesel engines, while the Eastern enterprise could specialize in certain labor-intensive components of the series. Another type of product-specialization agreement involves the production of different series of the same product. There is an agreement between Olympia-Werke of West Germany and Unis of Yugoslavia in which the Yugoslav enterprise will produce 250,000 typewriters a year, of which 200,000 are to be delivered to Olympia. There may also be production contracting of parts and components. These agreements represent a decision to narrow the range of components produced and to rely on contractual arrangements with partner firms for the remainder. Each partner can execute its particular part of the agreement, and the products can be exchanged to achieve a complementary production. Product-contract agreements may evolve further into coproduction and product-specialization agreements, involving two-way commitments and resulting flows of goods and services.

Joint-Marketing Agreements

Joint-marketing agreements are usually linked to licensing or franchising arrangements or to joint-production agreements. There also could be the formation of a joint-marketing company. Because of inadequate socialist marketing skills and contacts in the West, the marketing expertise of Western firms is quite important. The marketability of Eastern products in Western markets is greatly enhanced by direct marketing links with Western firms. A Western firm can see to it that the Eastern product conforms to Western market specifications and quality standards. The use of Western brand names and trademarks also improves the acceptance of Eastern products marketed in the West. Moreover, the Western firm in the marketing agreement, as end-user or as direct distributor, constitutes a built-in market for the Eastern product or products in the West. Thus, the Eastern firm is provided with a stable and long-term market. The Eastern partner also gains not only exclusive marketing rights to the product within its domestic territory but often gains exclusive or non-exclusive rights in other areas as well, especially within Eastern Europe.

One example of a joint-market agreement is incorporated in a production venture between a Dutch shipyard and a Polish foreign-trade organization. In 1977 the Dutch shipbuilding firm IHC signed a contract with Poland's Navimor Foreign Trade Organization to supply two bucket dredges for use in the Polish port city of Gdansk. In return a Polish shipyard chosen by Navimor will produce IHC–designed dredging barges, which IHC will sell to contractors and port authorities throughout Europe. The Polish-made barges will be sold under the trademark of the Dutch company but will carry the name of the Polish shipyard. In this example the Western partner provides its marketing expertise in Europe to sell the output of the Eastern enterprise.

There can also be marketing agreements to sell in the West technology developed in a socialist country. In some cases Eastern foreign-trade organizations have formed joint-trading companies with Western industrial partners. These companies can share joint equity in terms of legal arrangements. Their purpose is to improve the marketability of Eastern products by raising their technical standards, adapting them more closely to Western requirements, and promoting them more intensively within the Western market area. One example of a joint-trading company involves the Hungarian foreign-trade organization, Hungarotex, which has formed joint-marketing ventures with companies in Spain, the United States, and West Germany for the purpose of marketing Hungarian textiles and ready-to-wear clothing in Western markets. *

The Pepsi-Cola Corporation agreement with the Soviet Union illustrates a tie-in between joint-marketing and joint-production agreements. A high-speed bottling plant was installed by Pepsi-Cola in the Soviet Union, which produced 50 million bottles of Pepsi in 1976. Pepsi-Cola furnished the Soviets with the essentials for making Pepsi, including bottling equipment from West Germany, over a five-year period. Pepsi-Cola is responsible for quality control, but the Soviets are responsible for the operation of the plant and the distribution of the product. The cola concentrate is provided by Pepsi-

---

*The Romanian joint company Arcode operates in England to sell products made by Romanian enterprises to British distributors and consumers and is thus able to penetrate the local markets.

Cola under a barter arrangement in which Pepsi-Cola has the right to sell Soviet vodka and wine in the United States. The more vodka and wine Pepsi sells in the United States, the more Pepsi concentrate the Soviets get in return. Probably the single most important factor in the agreement is the marketing expertise provided by Pepsi-Cola, including the commercials it furnishes for Soviet television. The agreement has enabled Pepsi to gain an entrance into the markets of other Eastern bloc countries and has established a pattern for future arrangements in the developing market for Western consumer goods in Eastern Europe. In fact, Pepsi-Cola has attained a monopoly in the distribution of soft drinks in much of Eastern Europe.

Licensing Agreements

Licensing makes available to a foreign firm some intangible industrial property such as a patent, a manufacturing process, or a trademark for the purpose of cultivating the foreign licensee's market. This obviates the licenser company's need for entering the foreign licensee's market through export trade or direct capital investment. Licensing agreements also provide an inexpensive means for exploring and testing a company's growth potential in a particular foreign area before any irretrievable investment is made. From a risk standpoint licensing agreements entail a greater risk than normal export operations but considerably less risk than direct investments. For this reason licensing is frequently used as a transitional phase between export and foreign manufacture in a company's international expansion process and is succeeded by a more extensive commitment. In return for property rights transferred to it, the foreign licenser pays royalties normally based on its output or sales of the licensed product. In some cases licensing agreements may provide for a low or declining royalty plus a stock purchase commitment in a new or existing company to succeed the licensing arrangement. This, however, would not be applicable to licensing agreements with socialist enterprises.

One merit of a licensing agreement, as far as the socialist countries are concerned, is that it does not have to involve payments of royalties to Western firms, with a resulting drain on hard currency in the socialist country. A Western firm can agree to take part of the product licensed. For example, there is an agreement between the Swedish firm Ericsson and a Polish state enterprise in which the latter is licensed to produce relay devices for railway signal boxes.[5] The agreement requires the Polish state enterprise to pay one-half of the license fees in the form of delivery of these devices to the Swedish company. La Précision Industrielle, a French manufacturer of highly specialized machine tool equipment, signed a licensing agreement with Hungary's Licensia for the production of hydraulic trucks.[6] In another agreement, under which a Polish agricultural machinery plant is to produce heavy tractors licensed by International Harvester, part of the product is to be marketed in other countries on a joint basis. Reverse licensing from East to West also occurs. A Swedish company has begun production, under Soviet license, of installations for specialized equipment for electrohydraulic casting, imported from the Soviet Union.[7] Hungarian enterprises have established joint companies with Western European partners to produce medical equipment under license.

Licensing involves a continuous cooperative relationship between two parties for their mutual benefit. It is correct to classify licensing as a nonequity joint venture where pooling of resources between the partners is the overriding consideration. Licensing agreements are generally easier to negotiate and arrange than the more complex forms of industrial cooperation. The price of a license may be calculated either as a fixed sum to be paid in installments or as a royalty based on sales or production. Licensing provides an easy way to attain market penetration, since little or no outlay of capital is required. But there are also some disadvantages. Eastern European licensees generally want to buy the patent along with the license and know-how. This can be a costly affair, because one machine may require the registration of many patents. As patent fees rise for each additional year of registration—and patent administration costs are also involved —it can all add up to substantial sums. Moreover, studies have shown that earnings from licensing agreements are generally lower in comparison with other forms of joint-venture arrangements, especially during the rapid growth stage of the produce life cycle.[8]

Project Agreements

The project agreement differs from the joint-production venture in terms of the vast outlay of money and the scope of activities involved. Fiat, the Italian automotive firm, constructed the $800 million Togliatti automotive factory in the Soviet Union. The West German firm Salzgitter concluded several arrangements with the Soviet Union providing for the delivery of chemical plants and machinery for Soviet metallurgy. When a complete plant or production line is delivered, there is, in effect, a transfer of technology whose price is normally included in the price of the facility or equipment. The supplier may be responsible for training personnel as well as starting up the plant. The project agreement may provide for payment or partial payment in the products of the plant. For example, one project agreement between Salzgitter and the Soviet Union called for German purchases of polyethylene produced in the Soviet Union by low-density polyethylene plants installed by the firm. As a result of the project agreements concluded by Salzgitter with the Soviet Union, the firm and related subsidiaries were committed to purchase DM600 million worth of products from the plants constructed in the Soviet Union.

Of considerable potential importance to the United States is the formation of the Yakutia gas consortium in which two U.S. firms, El Paso Natural Gas Company and Occidental Petroleum, have entered into a general agreement with the Tokyo Gas Company to join the Soviet Union in exploring the natural gas reserves of the Yakutsk River in Eastern Siberia. [9] The agreement, which was contingent upon successful exploration for gas reserves, would eventually lead to the construction of pipelines, liquefaction plants, and port facilities in the Soviet Union. Under the terms of the agreement, the Soviet Union is supposed to supply natural gas from the Yakutia fields to the United States and Japan at an annual rate of 10 billion cubic meters beginning in 1983. The gas is to be transported by a 4,250 kilometer pipeline to the Soviet port of Murmansk for shipment to Philadelphia, from which it is to be transported to U.S. plants by the El Paso Natural Gas Company.

In November 1976 the Soviet Union began the exploration of natural gas deposits in southern Yakutia in conjunction with the El Paso Natural Gas Company, Occidental Petroleum, and the Tokyo Gas Company. [10] The U.S. and Japanese firms provided the equipment and technical services. The $100 million cost of the exploration is financed 50 percent by the Soviet Union, 25 percent by a credit provided by the Bank of America, and an equal amount provided by the Eximbank of Japan. Under the terms of the agreement, the Soviets are supposed to purchase $3.6 billion in equipment and expertise from the United States. This is contingent upon the Soviet Union's obtaining U.S. loans. However, the United States has told the Soviets that it is not in a position to discuss Eximbank financing because official credits to the Soviet Union are cut off by law. The repayment of the loan would be made by the Soviets through the sale of natural gas to the United States.

The implications of project agreements are significant. Because of the vast outlay of capital and the scope of activities involved, they require the participation of very large multinational corporations or consortia of a number of them. Moreover, since these agreements involve large deferred payments beyond the capacity of multinational corporations to finance, they require financing from large banks or export credit institutions. There is something inherent in the nature of doing business with a centrally planned economy that may well lead to greater industrial concentration in the West. In the initial stage of industrial cooperation with the Soviet Union and the other planned economies of Eastern Europe, it has usually, but not always, been the larger Western companies that have made the project agreements and been willing to take the risks. To a considerable degree, large companies such as the El Paso Natural Gas Company and Occidental Petroleum have the resources, capital, and initiative to facilitate the handling of multimillion dollar joint projects. They also have the credit and leverage with the large global banks that, if anything, have more economic power than the multinational industrial companies.

Subcontracting

Another form of industrial-cooperation agreement between Western enterprises and Eastern foreign-trade organizations and state enterprises involves a subcontracting arrangement in which a Western firm, confronted with a short- or medium-term shortage in production, subcontracts out production runs to Eastern firms with excess capacity. Subcontracting is of some importance in industrial-cooperation arrangements with Hungarian, Polish, and Yugoslavian state enterprises. In Hungary subcontracting in cutting and finishing clothes for Western markets is an important device for earning foreign exchange. Estimated Hungarian revenue from subcontracting agreements with Western firms amounted to $175 million in 1975. [11] In Yugoslavia and Poland subcontracting agreements are used in the rubber, iron and steel, footwear, and furniture industries. Poland has a number of subcontracting agreements with West German firms to supply parts and components. Most subcontracting agreements are for short-time periods, and typically the transfer of technology from West to East is negligible. Although subcontracting can be profitable to both Western and Eastern enterprises in the short run, it is not regarded as a particularly useful form of industrial cooperation for a longer period of time by most socialist countries.

Joint-Tendering Agreements

One form of East-West industrial cooperation that is becoming increasingly more frequent is the joint-tendering agreements for the construction of complete plants or processing lines or the undertaking of large civil engineering projects. The agreements are different from other forms of industrial cooperation in that they involve both Eastern and Western partners in the development of projects in a third country. There are several types of projects that can develop under joint tendering. A Western firm can subcontract to an Eastern state enterprise to build a plant or facility in Africa. For example, the West German Uhde-Siemens chemical consortium has signed an agreement with the Polimex Foreign Trade Organization of Poland to supply a chemical plant in Morocco. Polimex has delivered a sulfuric acid still, and the Uhde-Siemens consortium has delivered a reduction facility for the plant that will produce phosphoric acid. The Polish firm Polimex-Cekop and the French firm Entreprise Minière et Chimique signed a contract with the Indian government to deliver equipment and machines to be used in a chemical fertilizer complex in West Bengal. The contract also provides for the delivery of a complete fertilizer plant of French design and a complete soda plant of Polish design.

In the joint-tendering agreement, it is usually assumed that the Western firm is the senior partner and the Eastern firm is the junior partner. The implication is that the technology of the West is superior and that the Western firm contracts with an Eastern counterpart to contribute to the building of a plant or to the provision of machinery or equipment. This is not always the case, for the socialist partner can be the main contractor in a joint-tendering agreement. The Romanian foreign-trade enterprise Petrom and the West German conglomerate Buttner-Schilde-Haas contracted for the joint delivery of a polyacril-nitril fibers plant to North Korea, with Petrom serving as the main contractor and the German firm serving as the minor contractor and provider of machinery.

Other Forms of Industrial Cooperation

Industrial-cooperation agreements can also involve research and development of products in process. One example is the General Electric agreement with the Soviet Union concerning joint research and development on electric power generating equipment. Under joint research and development agreements, there can be provision for joint commercial rights to sell products or process technology developed. Then there is the turnkey agreement in which a Western firm constructs a plant for an Eastern country. Voest-Alpine, an Austrian firm, built a turnkey chemical plant in the German Democratic Republic (East Germany), using state enterprises as subcontractors. This turnkey arrangement developed into long-term industrial-cooperation agreements between the Austrian firm and East Germany, including joint-development projects in third countries. There are also franchise agreements in which a Western firm makes available to an Eastern partner technical and managerial assistance, training of personnel, and equipment. Land, labor, construction material, engineering, and technical services are provided by the Eastern partner. Hotels are a case in point. A number of different Western enterprises have entered into agreements for the construction of Intercontinental Hotels in Bucharest, Budapest, Prague, and Warsaw. Hilton International Hotels and Holiday Inn have made similar arrangements in several Eastern European countries.

Characteristics of Industrial Cooperation

The amount of East-West trade attributed to industrial cooperation is small in comparison with the total volume of East-West trade,
amounting to between 15 and 20 percent of the volume.[12] However,
the low proportion understates the significance of industrial cooperation in relation to East-West trade. Moreover, there is a considerable variation in the importance of the various types of industrial-
cooperation agreements. Coproduction and product-specialization
agreements account for over one-third of all industrial-cooperation
agreements between East and West. Licensing agreements are also
of importance, accounting for around 30 percent of the total number
of agreements. Licensing is often the first step toward the development of more complex industrial-cooperation arrangements between
the East and West partners. It is used in high-technology areas, thus
emphasizing the growing importance of the transfer of technology in
East-West trade.

Location of Industrial-Cooperation Agreements

The importance of industrial cooperation varies among countries. The countries that have concluded the greatest number of industrial-cooperation agreements with the West are the Soviet Union
and Poland, followed by Romania and Hungary.[13] It is estimated that
25 percent of all Hungarian products exported to the West result from
industrial-cooperation agreements.[14] The remaining countries, in
particular the German Democratic Republic, have far fewer cooperation agreements with the West. The Soviet Union, Poland, and Romania have the greatest number of agreements with U.S. firms. It
is necessary to remember, however, that this is not in dollar terms
but in the number of agreements. U.S. business relations with Poland can be explained by the long and stable political links that have
existed between the two countries, but the relationship with Romania
is more difficult to explain. One factor is Romania's determination
to be as independent of Soviet influence as possible. U.S. firms may
also find that cooperation with Romania can provide an additional
bonus—namely, an entry into the China market. Unlike the other
Eastern European countries, Romania has maintained cordial commercial and diplomatic relations with Peking, a fact not lost on U.S.
business firms. Romania also enjoys especially good political and
commercial relations with Third World countries.

Types of U.S. Cooperation Agreements

The two most common types of industrial-cooperation agreements into which U.S. firms have entered with Eastern partners are
licensing and turnkey arrangements. Of 267 agreements signed be-

tween U.S. firms and the East during the period between the fall of 1974 and the winter of 1975, 85 percent were of the licensing and turnkey types.[15] Both represent traditional areas in which U.S. business has demonstrated a capacity to perform, and both involve a transfer of technology. The turnkey arrangement is of particular importance in terms of monetary value to U.S. firms, since it involves more than delivery and assembly of machinery. It also involves the provision of designs, the training of personnel, and assistance in starting up and operating the plant. U.S. firms have an advantage over most Western European firms in the turnkey arrangement, because they are large enough to meet even the Soviets' great requirements for machinery and equipment. Licensing is, of course, an easy way in which to penetrate any foreign market. If successful with licensing, firms can proceed to more complicated forms of industrial cooperation. Other forms of industrial-cooperation agreements are of less importance to U.S. firms, indicating perhaps that they are mainly influenced by short-term considerations such as market penetration.

Industry Distribution of U.S. Cooperation Agreements

Technology-intensive industries play an important role in U.S. cooperation agreements with the East. The chemical industry accounted for around 21 percent of 439 industrial-cooperation agreements, followed by the machine tool industry with 20 percent, the electrical industry with 10 percent, and metallurgy with 6 percent.[16] By far the largest number of agreements involve investment-oriented projects and products and intermediate industrial goods, with a minority occurring in consumer-related industries. The industry distribution of these agreements varies from country to country, with the machine tool industry occupying first place in the number of agreements in Hungary and Romania.[17] In this industry it is possible to divide production operations into a set of component activities that can take place at separate locations. Parts and components for most equipment and machinery, for automobiles and other vehicles, and for most types of electrical consumer goods can be produced at separate locations and assembled elsewhere. Thus, the machine tool industry is ideally suited to the kind of international division of labor characteristic of industrial-cooperation agreements.

Size of U.S. Firms Involved
in Industrial Cooperation

On an a priori basis it can be assumed that the typical Western firm involved in industrial cooperation with Eastern firms would be multinational in its operations. After all, multinational firms have the world business contacts and an access to sources of credit not available to small firms. To a considerable degree they have the resources, and initiative to take advantage of business opportunities, as witnessed by Occidental Petroleum's business deals with the Soviet Union. They can take advantage of the economies of scale that large-volume production can offer. On the Eastern side state foreign-trade organizations, as opposed to individual state enterprises, are by far the most frequent partners and, in many cases, the only partners in East-West industrial-cooperation agreements. The foreign-trade organizations often show a predilection for dealing with large Western firms, particularly when expensive projects are involved. They can use the financial resources, technology, and marketing networks of the large multinationals. The monopolistic trade practices of the foreign-trade organizations can give Western multinationals exclusive long-term access to potentially large markets.

On balance multinationals account for a majority of the East-West industrial-cooperation agreements.[18] However, a much larger percentage of U.S. firms participating in these agreements would qualify as multinationals than is the case with Western European firms. In West Germany many medium-sized firms with primarily domestic markets are involved in cooperation agreements with the East. Of course, the geographic propinquity of West Germany to Eastern Europe would favor participation of German firms of all sizes in business arrangements with the East. As far as the United States is concerned, it is a different story. Industrial-cooperation agreements are heavily concentrated among the largest U.S. firms. Of the aforementioned 267 agreements concluded between U.S. firms and Eastern partners between the fall of 1974 and the winter of 1975, 189 were entered into by firms of Fortune's 500 select list of largest firms ranked by sales.[19] Some of these agreements were entered into by one firm. Tenneco, for example, has agreements with several Eastern European countries. In fact, nearly one-half of all U.S. firms engaged in East-West industrial cooperation have some type of involvement in more than one socialist country. There is something inherent in the nature of doing business with a nonmarket economy that may well lead to greater industrial concentration in the United States.

Countertrade

Methods of financing industrial-cooperation agreements can be complex.[20] A joint-production agreement consummated in a socialist country involves a Western firm in the currency of the country in which it is operating and an integration of its activity within the gen-

eral economic system of the country. The individual components of
the Western and Eastern partners' assets in an industrial-cooperation
agreement would be expressed in the currency of the Western partner
in prices agreed upon in the process of negotiation. A part of the contribution of the socialist partner can be evaluated in terms of its home
currency as a part of liquid working capital necessary for financing
such an operation. This part would be converted at the official bank
exchange rate used in the country of the Western partner and, when
expressed in the currency of the country, would be used in the accounting and cost projections used in the production agreement. Difficulties occur when expressing socialist production costs in Western
currencies. These are connected with the evaluation of a number of
cost elements and stem from socialist shortcomings in the definition
of costs.

The balance-of-payments problems of the socialist countries
present one of the greatest obstacles to the expansion of industrial
cooperation and trade. To ease this obstruction, the Eastern European countries have had recourse to hard-currency credits. Competition existed among Western creditors to extend loans to stimulate
exports or to extract concessions. But inflation, liquidity problems,
and high interest rates in the West have decreased the availability of
credit. Many Eastern European countries are now heavily in debt
but are still actively seeking new sources and types of credit. This
problem is further compounded by the difficulty in assessing their
reserve positions, levels of indebtedness, and future prospects for
hard-currency earnings. Lack of accurate financial disclosure makes
for a difficult determination of credit risk, as there is no reliable
balance-of-payments information to determine whether Eastern exports can increase more rapidly than indebtedness and whether hard
currency is available to service the debts. Many East-West cooperation agreements involve large long-term credit arrangements, which,
as a rule, are supported by Western government credit agencies,
thus minimizing risks of default.

As Eastern hard-currency indebtedness increased to an estimated $60 billion in 1978, so has the pressure to enter into agree-
ments whereby Western technology, plants, and facilities can be acquired without the eventual commitment of hard-currency reserves.[21]
In order to repay Western credit, the Eastern countries must generate hard currency through exports. Industrial-cooperation agreements
have come to include provisions for product purchase or exchange between Eastern and Western partners. These provisions come under
the category of countertrade, which can be defined as a set of transactions where the hard-currency claim on a socialist country resulting from an import from the West is offset by a balancing Western
purchase of Eastern products. Most Western equipment purchased by

the Eastern European countries under industrial-cooperation agreements is financed by Western credit. The Eastern European countries have to repay the credit and may insist on a counterarrangement in which Western firms agree to purchase or take goods from their Eastern partners. Countertrade can be divided into three types: simple barter agreements, buy-back or product pay-back agreements, and counterpurchase agreements. The characteristics of each are presented below.

Barter Agreements

Simple barter agreements involve a direct exchange of products and date back to the beginning of time. There is no money exchanged in a barter agreement, which is usually a one-shot proposition rather than a continuing relationship extending over a period of time. Its genesis in East-West trade developed in the early 1920s when a U.S. entrepreneur, Armand Hammer, who is currently chairman of the board of Occidental Petroleum, made an arrangement with Lenin to exchange U.S. grain for Soviet furs and caviar. More recently, Pepsi- Cola agreed to help build bottling plants in the Soviet Union and keep them supplied with the soft-drink syrup. In return for providing the syrup, Pepsi-Cola was given the exclusive right to market Stolichnaya vodka in the United States. Barter agreements work best when the products exchanged are of immediate benefit to their recipients. However, Western companies may find themselves with products that are difficult to market. For example, the West German Krupp conglomerate sold machine tools to Hungary in direct exchange for Hungarian cherry preserves, scouring pads, and pickles. Krupp experienced problems in trying to find markets for the Hungarian products but managed to sell them through a retail subsidiary.

Buy-Back Agreements

Buy-back agreements, or, as they are often called, compensation agreements, represent a much more sophisticated form of barter. They call for the Western partner in an industrial-cooperation agreement to build a production facility for the Eastern partner and then to purchase the resultant products. In May 1978 the French automotive firm Citroën announced that it would build a $368 million factory in East Germany and take full payment in the form of the front-wheel-drive transmissions the plant would make.[22] A major buy-back agreement was concluded between Occidental Petroleum and the Soviet Union in 1973.[23] It calls for the construction of eight ammonia plants and related facilities in the Soviet Union, financed partly by the Soviets and partly by Occidental Petroleum, which will purchase the end product for eventual sale in the West. In the buy-back type of agreement, both the Western and Eastern partners receive full payment for their transactions. The Western partner then contracts to buy the resultant products of the Eastern partner, which now has the money to pay off the loan to the Western bank. The Western firm is free to either use or sell the Eastern partner's product.

Counterpurchase Agreements

Counterpurchase agreements do not involve the acquisition of products derived from, or related to, a Western firm's commitment of technology, a plant, or equipment to a socialist partner but instead deal with unrelated or nonresultant products. In such agreements the Western firm may agree to market goods in fields that are unrelated to its own business. Daimler-Benz, the West German automotive company, exchanged 30 flatbed trucks with Romania in return for 150 jeeps.[24] Daimler-Benz then traded the jeeps to Ecuador for bananas, which were sold in West Germany to a supermarket chain. In this type of counterpurchase agreement, Daimler-Benz received only partial payment in cash and part in product, with full payment deferred until it was able to find a buyer for the Romanian product. This may be distinguished from another type of counterpurchase agreement in which cash payments are made in full at the time of product delivery by both the Western and Eastern enterprises. There is a quid pro quo relationship in that the Western firm's purchase of goods from the Eastern partner generates hard currency that is used by the latter to pay the Western firm. There are two separate contracts—one for the sale of Western products and a second for the purchase of Eastern products.

Eastern European countries are placing increased emphasis on counterpurchase agreements in order to alleviate hard-currency shortages. In Poland, for example, it is estimated that by 1980, 60 percent of all imports will be covered by counterpurchase agreements involving package deals wherein the Western seller has the option of selecting from an assortment of products, including textiles, chemicals, machinery, and other products.[25] Counterpurchase agreements are also widely used by the German Democratic Republic (East Germany).[26] Available are such products as optical equipment, diesel engines, sporting goods, machine tools, cranes, forklift trucks, and electronic components. The quality of many East German products is considered good by Western standards. In Hungary a Western firm is required to honor the counterpurchase agreement first and then deduct the proceeds it receives for the sale of Hungarian countertrade goods in the West from the price of goods delivered to Hungary. In the other Eastern European countries counterpurchase agreements vary in importance. Romania requires the highest percentage of counterpurchase for the goods it purchases in the West, and the prices of goods it offers are often higher than those of any other Eastern European country.[27]

Problems of Countertrade

Although countertrade is becoming a growing factor in East-West trade, the practice faces some serious limitations in terms of use. One such limitation involves the quality of the socialist products used in countertrade. Often these products fail to meet Western quality control and market standards. The quality defects of Eastern-manufactured goods are proverbial, on both sides of the line. However, the quality of products can vary from country to country. The Poles, under industrial-cooperation agreements, produce components that are used by such highly regarded Western manufacturers as Singer and Telefunken of West Germany. A Polish state enterprise manufactures Singer sewing machines under license and sells them in Poland under the Singer trademark, with the U.S. company paid entirely in Polish-made sewing machines. The Polish state enterprise Lodz Radio Works exchanges components for record players under license from Telefunken. The products from Czechoslovakia and Hungary, for the most part, are generally of high quality; with Bulgaria, Romania, and the Soviet Union, there are both limited choice and questionable quality of the goods available for countertrade.[28] Moreover, in all Eastern European countries there are problems with product delivery, availability of spare parts, and after-sale service.

Other limitations of Eastern European countertrade include an insufficient volume of desirable products that can be made available as counterdeliveries. Expanding domestic needs, together with trade commitments with developing countries and within the Council for Mutual Economic Assistance, may claim a significant amount of products that otherwise would be used as countertrade exports. There is also inefficient coordination of countertrade arrangements within each socialist country. In Romania, for example, contract negotiations are made difficult because a Western firm must deal with many diverse foreign-trade organizations, and the subject of counterpurchase may not come up until the end of the negotiations. Linkage among various classes of products available for export simply does not exist. Western firms with counterpurchase agreements in the Soviet Union find it impossible to purchase goods from any other foreign-trade organization except the one with which they are dealing. Western firms, in order to complete a deal, can find themselves in a situation where they agree to purchase a product without knowing what the market price for the product is in the West, or even if it is marketable in the West. Products accepted in counterpurchase may not be in the product line of a company.

One advantage of a countertrade agreement is that it can enable a Western firm to acquire access to sources of raw materials and industrial supplies. Both the Soviet Union and Poland have natural resources that are of importance to Western firms. Poland has an abundant supply of coal, which is in demand in the West. Poland has signed an agreement with Italy to supply coal in return for financial aid for expansion of its coal-mining industry. A somewhat similar agreement exists with the Netherlands. In an arrangement with a British firm, Poland has agreed to purchase an airline terminal complex to be built in Warsaw, with partial repayment made through a counterpurchase of construction material from Poland. The unlimited and virtually untapped natural resources of the Soviet Union provide a prime attraction for Western firms to engage in countertrade arrangements, particularly when there is a guarantee of a long-term supply. Natural gas is a case in point. However, the other Eastern European countries are reluctant to offer their raw materials as countertrade products, preferring to offer manufactured and semimanufactured products instead.

The success or failure of countertrade agreements can also depend on the economic health of the Western countries. During a period of recession in the West, the acquisition of Eastern goods by Western firms could result in lower profits if no markets can be found. Also, the more Eastern countries in which a Western firm becomes involved with respect to countertrade agreements, the more complex negotiations, financing, contracts, and repurchase arrangements become. Some countertrade agreements entail long-term requirements to purchase large volumes of goods. These agreements ensure the presence of Eastern goods in world markets over an extended period of time. The marketing of these goods is likely to have an effect on world markets. Since, for the most part, Eastern-return flows from countertrade agreements are only starting to appear in substantial volumes, it is difficult for Western firms to gauge the general impact that this trading mechanism will have on their own markets, in particular, and Western markets, in general. Western governments could conceivably intervene if local market disruptions occur from the importation of a wide variety of goods under countertrade agreements.

Countertrade agreements are a relatively recent development, and it is difficult to assess their profitability and desirability. It can be expected that countertrade will remain an important component of East-West commercial relations, particularly since hard-currency claims on the Eastern European countries are minimized. To some extent countertrade provides a crutch to compensate for the inability of the socialist countries to compete successfully with their exports in the world markets and, thus, earn hard currency. It appears likely that the Eastern European countries will continue to press for countertrade agreements, particularly of the compensation type in which a Western firm usually purchases products derived directly from, or produced by, Western-supplied technology, plants, or equipment. Countertrade is also compatible with state economic planning because it is self-liquidating, thus helping to moderate shifts in exports and allowing the formulation of long-term trade plans.

A number of U.S. companies have indicated that they do not consider engaging in countertrade, particularly counterpurchase agreements.[29] A major reason is that the size of the counterpurchase and the prospective profit margin are in many cases too small to justify the managerial effort required to consummate the transaction. Often negotiations between U.S. firms and socialist foreign-trade organizations break down because firms refuse to consider a counterpurchase agreement. In part this reluctance is attributable to the fact that many of the goods offered by the socialist foreign-trade organization are often not suitable for sale in U.S. and other Western markets due to a variety of factors—poor quality, design, packaging, service, and lack of brand-name recognition. In some cases U.S. firms have evinced an interest in counterpurchase or buy-back agreements if the product could be used within the company, but this often proves to be impossible. A large U.S. computer-manufacturing company expressed a willingness to engage in a counterpurchase agreement with the Soviet Union but found that it had extreme difficulty in finding anything that could be used in its operations.[30]

In areas where there is competition, U.S. and Western European firms are more likely to accept some form of countertrade agreement. For example, there has been an especially strong demand in Eastern Europe for agricultural and construction machinery, including tractors, and Western firms are less able to resist some form of countertrade, knowing that if they do, competitors may accept. U.S. agricultural and construction equipment companies active in Eastern European trade vary in their attitudes toward countertrade.[31] One well-established multinational corporation has agreed in principle to counterpurchase Eastern European products, but not in specific amounts, and only if company specifications are met.[32] Another company agreed to take 50 percent of payment in Eastern products but found that desired items could not be supplied with service. Designs were superseded, and the host country components no longer fit the U.S. company's latest models. The company found its small size to be a disadvantage; it lacked the capacity to absorb and distribute the products taken in the counterpurchase agreement. Other companies have been more successful in entering into countertrade agreements. They perceive a maximum gain from involvement with Eastern state enterprises and are willing to accept Eastern products as a condition for doing business.

A problem that can face U.S. firms inexperienced in the process of countertrade is that they may not realize that their sales are attached, say, to a counterpurchase agreement until terms and prices have been negotiated. When negotiations are time-consuming to begin with, and when sales contracts are completed, it is possible for U.S. firms to be in a position of having to agree to accept counterpurchases to consummate the sales process. This can create a problem, because a U.S. firm can be put in the position of having to accept a product without knowing whether there is a market for it in the West. There is, of course, a European-broker network that can expedite the disposal of counterpurchase goods, usually at a discount of anywhere from 10 percent to 20 percent of the normal sales price of the goods in Western European markets. Western European firms also possess an advantage over U.S. firms because they have been involved in counterpurchase agreements over an extended period of time. Many have divisions expert in this kind of trading; others rely on the numerous traders who specialize in it.

SUMMARY

Industrial cooperation within the East-West trade rubric can be defined as a set of economic activities and relationships arising from contracts that may extend over a number of years between partners belonging to different economic systems. These contracts go far beyond the simple export or import of goods and services; instead, they involve a set of complementary or reciprocally matching arrangements in production, in the development and transfer of technology, and in marketing. These arrangements can involve the mutual pooling of assets, both tangible and intangible. There may or may not be formal equity links between the partners. Industrial cooperation also involves a complex set of property rights that create an interdependence among Eastern and Western firms that is different from the interdependence generated through market relations. There is a by-passing of the impersonal pricing mechanism in favor of a more direct interfirm agreement. Cooperation agreements involve a broader spectrum of activities than do market transactions and may extend to activities, such as research and development, that are not directly market related.

There are various types of industrial cooperation ranging from joint-equity ventures to industrial-cooperation agreements. In the joint-equity venture, two partners pool their assets to form a new and distinct business entity. There is a property relationship flowing from equity ownership; the partners agree to share profits and losses and jointly manage the entity. However, joint-equity ventures are not frequently used in Eastern Europe, as most socialist countries do not permit their formation. More common forms of industrial cooperation include coproduction and specialization agreements. In these agreements the East and West partners produce components for a final product to be assembled by one partner. The technology is supplied by one partner, and there is usually an agreement to market the product in each partner's respective market. Licensing agreements are a common type of industrial cooperation. A Western firm may license the use of its technology to a socialist partner. Payment for the use can be made in products or components or in hard-currency royalties. One merit of a licensing agreement is that it provides an easy way to penetrate socialist markets. It can also lead to other forms of industrial-cooperation agreements.

Subcontracting is another type of industrial-cooperation agreement. In subcontracting a socialist partner produces components or parts according to the specifications of the Western partner and delivers them to the Western partner. Subcontracting may also work in reverse. Western and Eastern partners can also contract for the delivery of a turnkey plant to a third country. In the turnkey arrangement one partner may supply the plant, while the other partner may supply equipment. Although the major part of the turnkey plant is usually supplied by the Western partner, this does not always have to be the case. Other types of industrial cooperation include joint-marketing agreements in which Eastern and Western partners agree to market each other's products in the home markets or in the market of a third country. There can also be franchising of trademarks and marketing know-how. Joint-research and -development projects are still another form of industrial cooperation. There is the coordinated implementation of research and development projects, with provision for joint commercial rights to all product or process technology developed under the agreement.

The term countertrade is generally used to describe all forms of East-West transactions under which the Eastern European buyer or partner requires a Western seller or partners to accept full or part payment in local products. The socialist countries have come to rely more on countertrade as a means of preserving their reserves of hard currency. There are several types of countertrade agreements. Barter involves a direct exchange of goods between an Eastern and Western partner, with no money and no third partner involved in the transaction. A second type of arrangement involves product buy-back. The Western firm that provides technology to an Eastern enterprise agrees to accept products made from the technology as partial payment. Then there is the counterpurchase agreement, which is the most common form of countertrade. The counterpurchase agreement involves two separate contracts that are linked together.

One is for the sale of the Western product and the other involves a commitment by a Western firm to purchase Eastern products in a value equal to a certain share of the sale of the Western product. An advantage of the counterpurchase agreement is that a Western firm can get full cash payment for its deliveries, while it has to pay for its own purchases only when suitable Eastern European products have been found.

NOTES

1. The most commonly accepted definition of industrial cooperation is the report of the United Nations' Economic Commission for Europe called the Analytic Report on Industrial Cooperation among ECE Countries.

2. Henry Z. Horbaczewski, "Profitable Coexistence: The Legal Foundation for Joint Enterprises with U.S. Participation in Poland," Business Lawyer 31 (November 1975): 433-55.

3. Martin Schnitzer, Contemporary Government and Business Relations (Chicago: Rand McNally, March 1978), p. 254.

4. Ibid., p. 254.

5. Business International, Business Eastern Europe, January 7, 1976.

6. Chase World Information Corporation, East-West Markets, July 25, 1977.

7. Ibid., July 11, 1977.

8. S. Benjamin Prasad and Y. Krishna Shetty, An Introduction to Mutlinational Management (Englewood Cliffs, N.J.: Prentice-Hall, 1976), p. 180.

9. U.S., Senate, Committee on Foreign Relations, U.S. Trade and Investment in the Soviet Union and Eastern Europe: Staff Report for the Subcommittee on Multinational Corporations, 93rd Cong., 2d sess., 1974, p. 20.

10. Chase World Information Corporation, East-West Markets, July 25, 1977.

11. Hungarian Chamber of Commerce, Hungarian Foreign Trade, no. 1 (1976), p. 10.

12. U.S., Senate, Committee on Finance, Multinational Corporations in the Dollar Revaluation Crisis: Report on a Questionnaire, Staff Report of the Subcommittee on Multinational Corporations, 94th Cong., 1st sess., 1975, pp. 1-31.

13. Paul I. McCarthy, "The U.S. Role in East-West Industrial Cooperation: A Comparison with the West European Experience" (Report prepared for the Bureau of East-West Trade of the U.S. Department of Commerce, Washington, D.C., 1975), p. 19.

14. Paul Marer, "Hungary's Industrial Cooperation with the West: Achievements, Problems, and Perspectives" (Paper prepared for the Hungarian-U.S. Economic Council, U.S. Chamber of Commerce, Washington, D.C., 1976).

15. McCarthy, U.S. Role, p. 21.

16. Ibid., p. 32.

17. Ibid., p. 71.

18. U.S., Joint Economic Committee, "East-West Industrial Cooperation," in Eastern European Economies Post Helsinki, prepared by Carl H. McMillan, 95th Cong., 1st sess., 1977, p. 1189.

19. McCarthy, U.S. Role, p. 75.

20. U.S., Department of Commerce, East-West Countertrade Practices: An Introductory Guide for Business, prepared by Pompiliu Versariu, Scott Bozek, and Jenelle Matheson (Washington, D.C.: Government Printing Office, August 1978).

21. Business Week, November 10, 1978, p. 7.

22. Business Eastern Europe, October 8, 1978.

23. Occidental Petroleum, Annual Report to the Stockholders 1974, p. 5.

24. U.S., Joint Economic Committee, "Countertrade Practices in Eastern Europe," in Eastern European Economies Post Helsinki, prepared by Jenelle Matheson, Paul McCarthy, and Steven Flanders, 95th Cong., 1st sess., 1977, p. 1305.

25. Business International, "Current Countertrade Policies and Practices in East-West Trade," Multiclient research study completed November 1976.

26. Joseph Mandato, Thomas J. Skola, and Kenneth L. Wyse, "Counterpurchase Sales in the German Democratic Republic," Columbia Journal of World Business, Spring 1978, pp. 82-88.

27. Ibid., p. 85.

28. U.S., Department of Commerce, East-West Countertrade Practices, pp. 24-33.

29. Mandato, Skola, and Wyse, "Counterpurchase Sales," p. 87.

30. Ibid., p. 88.

31. John B. Holt, "Industrial Cooperation in Eastern Europe: Strategies of U.S. Agricultural and Construction Equipment Companies," Columbia Journal of World Business, Spring 1977, pp. 80-89.

32. Ibid., p. 84.

4
INDUSTRIAL COOPERATION
IN POLAND

Poland, of all the Eastern European countries, has perhaps the most hospitable environment for industrial cooperation, at least as far as the United States is concerned. The political situation of Poland relative to that of the United States has remained relatively favorable to industrial cooperation among business enterprises of the two countries. Poland offers the same attractions to U.S. and other Western firms as the other Eastern European countries, namely, a relatively low-paid labor force that includes skilled technical personnel and a degree of concentration in industry that allows for very large-scale operations. However, unlike other socialist countries, there is less institutional hostility to nonsocialist property. Although the Polish constitution asserts that the national economy is to be based on socialist modes of production, protection is also provided for private individual property. The Polish economy contains a sizable private sector, particularly in agriculture, where most land and farms are privately owned, but extends to other areas of economic activity as well.[1] There has also been a genuine desire on the part of the Polish government for more direct foreign involvement with the Polish economy.

In Poland, as is true in the other socialist countries of Eastern Europe, trade is a state monopoly. This means that U.S. and other Western firms interested in developing industrial-cooperation agreements with Polish state enterprises usually have to conduct arrangements through foreign-trade organizations, which are under the jurisdiction of the Ministry of Foreign Trade and Maritime Economy. In some cases direct enterprise-to-enterprise contact has been permitted, but state enterprises are granted a limited range of discretion in negotiation by the national economic plan. In this connection it is necessary to point out that industrial cooperation must be consistent with the priorities of the plan. Hard-currency constraints placed on state enterprises also inhibit their latitude in engaging in direct arrangements with Western enterprises. Often a state enterprise's foreign currency allotment may not be sufficient to cover those imports of machinery and equipment necessary to meet an industrial-cooperation agreement. Thus, responsibility for concluding industrial-cooperation agreements with U.S. and other Western firms lies with the Ministry of Foreign Trade and Maritime Economy, which has a bias toward agreements that lead to immediate export sales and against long-term production arrangements between the partners in the agreements.[2]

In terms of the number of industrial-cooperation agreements concluded with Western firms, Poland ranks second to Hungary; in terms of value of the agreements, Poland probably ranks first among the Eastern European countries.[3] Most Polish industrial-cooperation agreements with Western firms have been concluded in the 1970s and involve subcontracting, production-contracting, and licensing agreements. Licensing agreements with Poland have proved to be of particular advantage to Western firms, since abundant labor and natural resources combined with Western technology have resulted in production costs well below Western European levels. This factor has enhanced the marketing strategies of Western firms operating in Western and Eastern Europe. Polish foreign-trade enterprises have also been fairly active in joint-tendering agreements with Western firms in the developing countries. However, an adverse and continuing factor in Polish industrial-cooperation agreements with the West is the hard-currency deficit. This has increased government pressure to emphasize the self-financing aspects of industrial cooperation, despite Polish economists' recognition of a need to sacrifice short-term trade balance in the interest of improved long-term export performance.

THE LEGAL FRAMEWORK OF
INDUSTRIAL COOPERATION IN POLAND

Resolutions 314 and 159

Laws governing industrial-cooperation agreements between Polish state enterprises and Western firms date back to 1961, with Resolution 314 of the Council of Ministers.[4] Among other things the resolution permits state enterprises to enter into cooperation agreements with the approval of the appropriate ministry when the agreement is in the interest of the export trade, the domestic market, or the reduction of imports. These cooperation agreements could be extended to Western firms when it became necessary to meet quality standards or to ensure long-term sources of supply. The resolution defined in-dustrial cooperation as the supply of components necessary for the production of a specified final product on the basis of an agreement between two or more enterprises. The Council of Ministers has to consider the impact of any proposed change in the national economic plan on existing cooperation agreements. State enterprises could consider domestic and foreign cooperation agreements with both so-cialist and nonsocialist enterprises before making investment deci-sions and could create funds to finance these agreements. However, the use of these funds is subject to the approval of the State Planning Commission of the Council of Ministers.

Resolution 314 was amended by Resolution 159 of the Council of Ministers in 1971. The new resolution provided some important changes as far as industrial cooperation is concerned. Polish min-istries were given responsibility for securing the import of materials needed for production under industrial-cooperation agreements in which the Polish partner produces finished components or subcom-ponents; in such cases the foreign-exchange allotments of the minis-tries rather than the state enterprises are to be used. A special com-mission of high government officials was created to prepare annual recommendations for a sum to be included in the multiyear financial plans for investment in cooperative production. Premiums were au-thorized for the successful completion of industrial-cooperation agreements, and state enterprises whose production under the agree-ments exceed 50 percent of total output are put in a preferred class for receiving investment funds from the State Bank. It might be added parenthetically that managers of state enterprises that fail to perform creditably in a cooperation agreement can find themselves out of a job. Most state enterprises are granted a limited range of discretion by the economic plan and a severely restricted fund of convertible cur-rency. Thus, an agreement that goes sour may wipe out a state en-terprise's investment fund, leaving it without the means of making foreign purchases.

The basis of Polish industrial-cooperation agreements is a di-rect contract between both partners, which contains the subject mat-ter of the agreements, the quantities of cooperative components to be supplied in particular years, contract penalties, and procedures for amendment of the contract. [5] There is no special approval process, and foreign-trade enterprises can negotiate cooperation agreements on their own within the advisory framework of the Ministry of Foreign Trade and Maritime Economy. The agreements, of course, must fit within the constraints of the national economic plan. The provisions of the laws on special foreign currency and investment funds, contract priorities, and investment preferences and profit incentives as well

as the allowance of annual price revisions free Polish industrial-cooperation agreements from many of the strictures of the central planning system. Polish law makes it relatively attractive for state enterprises to enter into industrial-cooperation agreements and is designed to improve the possibility that they will be able to fulfill their
contractual obligations once an agreement has been concluded. In
this respect Polish law appears to be more flexible than either Romanian or Hungarian law.

Foreign Investments on Polish Soil

A decree of May 14, 1976, by the Council of Ministers allows
foreigners—both individual and corporate—to make direct investments
in Poland. [6] The decree, which stops short of permitting joint-equity
ventures, is designed to attract hard currency from the West. The
areas covered for direct foreign investments are crafts, internal
trade and catering services, hotel services, and other services. Licenses allowing foreigners and foreign companies to conduct business
on Polish soil have a life of up to ten years under the decree and can
be obtained from the Polish government, subject to the approval of
the Ministry of Foreign Trade and Maritime Economy or of the regional council director of the province in which the investment is to
be made. The key provisions for obtaining a license to operate in
Poland include the submission of an estimate of the investment required, the obligation to cover the cost of the investment in convertible
currency, and the deposit of 30 percent of the estimated investment
with the Polska Kasa Opieka ("Polish Savings Bank"). [7] No limits are
set on the amount of the investment, nor are there limits set on the
amount of ownership that can be held by foreigners.
    The decree of 1976 also deals with the repatriation of profits.
To repatriate profits, Polska Kasa Opieka is authorized to make convertible currency payments to foreign investors of up to 50 percent
of the net income derived in the fiscal year in an amount not to exceed 9 percent of the value of the investment deposit in convertible
currency. [8] No limitations on such payments are set where at least
50 percent of turnover in the sale of goods or services is effected
through documented sales against convertible currency. Further,
such payments may be made in cash, for transfer abroad or for transfer to the interest-bearing foreign currency account of the foreign
owner of an enterprise in Poland. Under specified conditions Polska
Kasa Opieka can transfer abroad a sum obtained by the owner of an
enterprise from its sale in entirety or in part, less the tax on the
sale. For converting earnings from investments in Poland into the
currency of the foreign firm doing the investment, special rates of

exchange fixed by the Polish State Bank Handlowy w Warszawicz, plus a premium applicable to the exchange of currency for foreign tourists, are used.

The decree, although it stops short of authorizing joint-equity ventures on Polish soil between Western firms and Polish state enterprises, opens the door for such a possibility. In theory Polish state enterprises are free to enter into joint-equity ventures on an ad hoc basis—that is, without a statute—as in Romania.[9] In practice there is the need to consider the theoretical as well as the mechanical problems of foreign-equity investment. Under the existing legal system, a company organized under the 1934 Commercial Code, in which state participation is greater than 50 percent, has the status of a state enterprise and, as such, enjoys special tax advantages over private enterprises. For example, the turnover tax on state enterprises is 4 percent on sales and 5 percent on services, with a complete exemption on commodities intended for export. These rates can be compared with much higher rates on sales and services for nonstate enterprises. State enterprises are exempt from the income tax, which can run as high as 65 percent, particularly for private entrepreneurs. Joint-equity participation with a state enterprise would give a foreign firm the same tax status.

Although foreign investment is permitted in Poland, it is necessary to point out that it is limited to certain small industries and service areas. These investments are encouraged to attract hard-currency funds from the Polish diaspora in the West and are linked to measures designed to encourage more domestic, private activities in consumer services. The need for hotels is a case in point. Poland, like other Eastern European countries, has a shortage of hotel accommodations, a factor that mitigates against the attraction of foreign tourists. Since foreign tourists are a prime source of hard currency, it is in the interest of the Polish economy to build facilities to attract them. The new investment regulations have attracted interest from foreigners planning to build hotels in Poland, in particular the Swedes. However, there is some dissatisfaction with the rules allowing direct foreign investment, since they were aimed primarily at the development of the service sector. One possible change is to further broaden the scope of the regulations to allow some foreign investments in the industrial sector of the Polish economy.

The significant degree of flexibility that Polish investment regulations provide indicates a pragmatic approach in attracting foreign business investment. This approach was influenced by Poland's continuing need for investment capital and new technology. To give foreign and Polish partners considerable latitude in setting up the organizational structure, while establishing legal guarantees for repatriation of profits and investment equity, is rather significant for a socialist country. How effective the new regulations are in attracting foreign capital to Poland remains to be seen. While there has been a considerable amount of foreign interest in the new regulations, which would certainly help problems of attracting hard currency and increasing productivity, so far little action has occurred. There is the question of how much it is worth to invest in Poland.

Many economists believe that the value of any investment depends upon the expectations of the stream of earnings it will produce in the future. In their view investors should pay no more than the sum of these earnings, after discounting them at some rate to reflect that money to be received in the future is worth less than money in the hand today. To so-called discount rate allows for what this money could earn if an investor had it now—which is close to 10 percent in the case of high-grade U.S. corporate bonds—and, in addition, compensates the investor for the greater risks of investments with less-certain payoffs than, for example, the high-grade bonds. If the discount method were used to determine whether to invest in Poland, a considerable degree of uncertainty as to earnings potential would have to be taken into consideration. There are probably better investment alternatives available, including the above-mentioned corporate bonds.

Foreign investment in Poland cannot depend more heavily on the possibility of capital appreciation than on future earnings—a possibility that is quite relevant to a capitalist country. Given the rate of inflation in Poland and elsewhere, determining the appropriate discount rates to use in capital gains calculations is also subject to some debate. A 10 percent rate of discount, many economists would agree, is too low since an investment in Poland is a riskier move than investing in something like high-grade corporate bonds. A higher rate should be used after factoring in the liquidity risks of foreign investment in Poland. The current Polish regulations designed to attract foreign investment are something new, untried, and unfamiliar. Goals and objectives have to be changed in a dynamic environment. The political situation is a critical factor, because if good relations are maintained between East and West, it could augur well for increased business investment in Poland.

The problems associated with the type of foreign business ventures that the new investment laws are trying to encourage are formidable. One basic problem with any type of venture project in Poland is the amount of time needed to consummate the project. A second problem is the amount of capital required. These and other problems may limit investment to the large foreign multinationals, since they are in a better position than smaller firms to enter into negotiations and to weather the vagaries of economic change. The new foreign investment rules may not make a significant contribution to solving Polish hard-currency problems, nor can they be counted on to increase productivity and efficiency in the service areas.

POLISH INDUSTRIAL-COOPERATION
AGREEMENTS WITH THE WEST

Poland ranks high in terms of the number of industrial-cooperation agreements concluded with the West. Growth occurred princi-
pally in the 1970s as Poland placed a high priority on policies designed
to modernize the economy and to improve the standard of living. The
Edward Gierek government believed in a growth imperative, for the
rate of economic growth was steadily falling behind that of the developing Eastern European countries that had begun modernization programs in the 1960s. Economic policy initiatives were developed that
aimed at the concomitant goals of rapid industrialization and sharply
rising living standards. To help achieve these goals, Poland imported
massive amounts of Western technology and equipment, aided by in-
fusions of readily attainable credit from the West. Industrial-cooperation agreements with Western firms were also encouraged by the
Gierek government. A number of measures were taken in Poland to
encourage domestic industrial and commercial enterprises to develop
cooperative ties with Western firms, including the relaxation of regulations for obtaining approval from the appropriate ministry or foreign-trade organization. The existence of laws favorable to industrial-cooperation agreements is an advantage to Western negotiators;
the substantive provisions bear the imprimatur of the Council of Ministers.

The Sources of Industrial-Cooperation Agreements

Poland's industrial cooperation with the Western capitalist countries developed in the early 1960s. The French were among the first
to enter into cooperation agreements with Poland when the automotive
firm Berliet, which is a part of the Regie-Renault conglomerate,
agreed to coproduce trucks and buses in Poland. In fact most commercial buses in Poland are produced from a factory built by Berliet
that originally cost around $80 million. Together with Saviem, an-
other Renault-owned truck manufacturer, Berliet also built a plant
to turn out trucks for consumption in Poland and for export to other
Eastern European markets. However, the French presence in Poland
is small in comparison with other Western capitalist countries. As
Table 3 indicates, Italy, West Germany, and the United States have
the greatest percentage of industrial-cooperation agreements with
Poland. The most important arrangement between Poland and Italy
involves industrial-cooperation agreements between Fiat and Pol-
Mot, the Polish automotive foreign trade organization. These agreements involve the production of Fiat cars in Poland, imports and as-

TABLE 3

Industrial-Cooperation Agreements between Poland and Selected
Capitalist Countries
(expressed as a percentage of all agreements)

Country	Cooperation-Related Exports	Cooperation-Related Imports
Italy	39	50
West Germany	32	22
United States	13	10
Sweden	3	8
France	2	7
Great Britain	2	2
Others	9	1
Total	100	100

Source: Witold Trzeciakowski, "Polish Experiences in East-West Industrial Cooperation" (Report prepared for the Foreign Trade Research Institute, Warsaw, Poland, July 1976).

sembly of the Fiat, and subcontracting of parts to be used in Fiat assembly plants in Italy. The set of agreements with Fiat is reflected in Italy's share of total agreements.

West Germany is also important in terms of the number of industrial-cooperation agreements concluded with Poland. In fact West Germany is Poland's largest Western trading partner, accounting for about one-fourth of the Polish trade deficit with the West. Polish industrial cooperation with West Germany takes a number of forms, the most important of which involve subcontracting for German firms and licensing. In subcontracting emphasis has been placed upon the production of parts and components, particularly in such areas as metallurgy, electrical equipment, chemicals, and transportation equipment. The majority of subcontracting agreements with West Germany are concluded for a brief period of time with small or medium-sized firms and are low in monetary value. In licensing Knorr-Bremse of Munich, one of Europe's largest manufacturers of automobile and locomotive brakes and power-steering devices, has been involved in several agreements with Poland. The

Polish state enterprise Lodz Radio Works manufactures components for record players under a license from the West German electronic firm Telefunken, which also has an agreement with the Polish enterprise Polar to purchase Polish absorption aggregates for use in its refrigerators. Grundig and Krupp have a similar arrangement with a Polish firm, receiving payment in Polish-made tape recorders.

Industrial-Cooperation Agreements
with the United States

Industrial cooperation, as defined previously, goes far beyond simple export-import transactions. It includes all forms of technology transfers—licensing, turnkey projects, coproduction, subcontracting, joint tendering, and joint ventures. In 1975, according to one source, there were 74 industrial-cooperation agreements either in force or in the process of being completed between U.S. firms and Polish state enterprises and foreign-trade organizations. [10] An additional 55 agreements were in various stages of negotiations. Of the 74 industrial-cooperation agreements, 62 involved firms listed in Fortune's 500 select list of the largest industrial firms, illustrating the point that, in Poland and in other Eastern European countries, it is the large U.S. multinational corporation that is most likely to be engaged in industrial cooperation. [11] This can be attributed in part to the fact that there are high costs and risks in entering socialist markets—costs, because negotiations require a considerable amount of time to consummate; risks, because there are uncertainties about how to negotiate and penetrate an Eastern market. There is also a preference on the part of the Poles and other Eastern Europeans to deal with U.S. corporations that are known world leaders in technology and have worldwide marketing networks. Many of the large U.S. firms with cooperation agreements in Poland also have agreements in other Eastern European countries.

Furthermore, some of the U.S.-Polish cooperation agreements can involve a considerable amount of money. Examples of industrial-cooperation agreements that are of large monetary value include the Corning Company-RCA and International Harvester agreements, both of which are discussed in more detail below. Corning is building a glass bulb plant and RCA a picture tube plant, the combined cost of which amounts to $125 million and is a result of competitive bidding from Western firms that had the technology to satisfy Polish requirements. The International Harvester agreement involves the production of crawler tractors and other construction machinery in Poland. In both examples the U.S. firms are representative of large U.S. multinationals in that they are financially strong, are leaders in technology, and have large marketing distribution networks. These companies also have cooperation agreements with other Eastern European countries.

Licensing and turnkey agreements accounted for well over half of the 74 U.S.-Polish industrial-cooperation agreements. [12] There were 26 licensing agreements, and most called for payment in products. For example, an agreement was signed by Westinghouse for the sale to Poland of licenses and equipment for semiconductors and rectifiers valued at $10 million. The Polish repayment was to be in semiconductors and rectifiers. Turnkey arrangements of various types accounted for 22 agreements. The Corning-RCA agreement involves a turnkey project. More than 50 technicians and managers have been directly involved in the project, many of whom have lived in Poland for various periods since it started. Again, it is the large U.S. firm that can provide the necessary resources to construct a turnkey facility of the size Corning and RCA are building in Poland. Coproduction and subcontracting agreements accounted for most of the remaining agreements. Most of the agreements were concluded in the following industrial categories: agricultural machinery and transportation equipment, electrical machinery and electronics, chemicals, nonelectrical machinery, and metallurgy. Nonelectrical machinery, as a manufacturing category, accounted for 14 of the total 74 agreements, while chemicals and electrical equipment agreements accounted for 5 each. [13] Some of the agreements involve cooperation in more than one product group, particularly where subcontracting is used.

RCA and Corning-UNITRA Agreement

One of the largest industrial-cooperation agreements ever concluded in Poland involves the U.S. firms Corning and RCA and UNITRA, the Polish foreign-trade organization that is responsible for the development of the state electronic industry. [14] The agreement, supported by Export-Import Bank (Eximbank) financing, is designed to provide the construction of a plant complex at Iwiczna that will product 21-inch, 110-degree precision, in-line color television picture tubes. The facility is comprised of a tube assembly plant and production lines for deflector components, electric guns, and phosphors. Its initial production is 300,000 tubes per year and is eventually to be increased to 600,000 per year. The agreement grants UNITRA exclusive licensing under Corning and RCA patents for the manufacture and sales of the tubes and glass envelopes in Poland and nonexclusive licenses outside of Poland. The Poles have created a state enterprise, Polcolor, to manufacture color television sets and picture tubes. It will operate four divisions—the Warsaw Television

Works, the plant at Iwiczna that will manufacture components, a picture tube factory, and a research and development center for vacuum technology. Sales within Eastern Europe and pricing are solely the responsibility of the Polish foreign-trade organization UNITRA.

The RCA part of the agreement provides technical assistance in the construction and design of plant facilities and installation of production equipment. RCA will also supply manufacturing know-how and equipment for producing the tubes and will train UNITRA personnel. It will continue to provide technical assistance to the Poles for a period of ten years, including help in the manufacture of color television receivers. Corning's part in the agreement is to construct a plant to produce glass envelopes for the color television tubes. Its responsibilities also include specification of all building, services, equipment, and materials, purchase or fabrication of most of the technical machinery and equipment, monitoring of the plant construction, detail supervision of the installation of production equipment, and supervising the start-up of the facility to a previously established level of production. The Corning portion of the agreement involves the moving of over 40 technical and manufacturing personnel to Poland. Some of the equipment to be supplied under the RCA-Corning contracts will be subcontracted from relatively small U.S. companies. There are contractual restraints to discourage Polish sale of the television products to the West.

W. R. Grace-WEGLOKOKS Agreement

Next to the United States, Poland is the largest coal-exporting country in the world. Through the state foreign-trade organization WEGLOKOKS, the country has exported 800 million tons of coal over a 20-year period. [15] Reconstruction of the Polish economy after World War II was facilitated to a major degree by income from coal exports. Poland did not succumb to predictions of the demise of coal as a world energy source. During almost worldwide exploration for oil, the Poles found new and larger beds of quality coal. While everyone else was turning to gas and oil, Poland was looking for ways to increase productivity of coal mines and coal use. Poland is one of the few countries that has an ample supply of energy. The foreign-trade organization WEGLOKOKS was created in 1952 to accomplish two goals: increase the volume and profitability of export sales of coal to earn foreign exchange and promote the development of international cooperation in solid-fuel research. It is responsible for the handling of all coal designated for export, from the time it leaves the ground to the time it is loaded aboard ship for final export destination.

In 1973 WEGLOKOKS entered into a joint-marketing agreement with W. R. Grace in which the latter agreed to serve as the exclusive

agent for Polish coal in the United States and Canada. Officials of
Grace and its subsidiary, Grace Ore and Mining, went to Poland in
1973 to conclude the agreement.[16] One basic reason for the agreement was the need for a cleaner energy source to produce electricity
in the United States. Most U.S. coal contains over 4 percent sulfur
dioxide, making it highly polluting. The Poles noted that U.S. en-
vironmental quality standards would force electric power companies
to switch to cleaner fuels such as gas and oil, or as a possible alternative, to import Polish coal, which has only a 0.7 percent sulfur
content. Thus, it was felt that there was a potential market for Polish
coal in the United States, but it was necessary to find a large U.S. company to provide the marketing expertise. WEGLOKOKS chose W. R.
Grace to market its coal in the United States because it is a multinational corporation with a worldwide distribution of chemical and consumer products and it also has natural resource interests. The sales
of Grace in 1973 amounted to $2 billion. Under the terms of the mar-
keting agreement, Grace agreed to the following terms and conditions:

1. Grace would arrange for ocean freight from Polish ports to
U.S. and Canadian ports. It would be responsible for insurance and
other necessary shipping arrangements.

2. It would find buyers in the United States and Canada for Polish coal and set the sales price.

3. It would receive a brokerage fee of 6 percent of the value
of each invoice, with a minimum brokerage fee of not less than 25
cents per ton of coal sold in the United States and Canada.

4. Payments to WEGLOKOKS would be made according to the
individual sales contracts. In the event that Grace invoiced the customer directly, payment would be made to the Polish foreign-trade
organization promptly after Grace's receipt of payment from the customer.

5. The agreement would be in effect for a period of three years;
after that time, it would be extended by mutual consent.[17]

International Harvester-BUMAR Agreement

International Harvester, a major U.S. multinational corporation
with manufacturing operations in 18 foreign countries,[18] entered into
an industrial-cooperation agreement with the Polish state construction
and agricultural machinery combine BUMAR Union to license the latter to manufacture crawler tractors and other types of construction
machinery. BUMAR, which is represented in foreign trade by the
foreign-trade organization BUMAR, produces 80 percent of Polish
heavy-duty construction machinery, a part of which is exported to
other countries.[19] The U.S. company was responsible for providing

technical advisers and training Polish technical personnel in the
United States. Compensation in the agreement involved a front-end
fee to International Harvester for the original technology, engineering,
and know-how package. In addition, there are research, engineering,
and manufacturing fees or royalties that are provided on an ongoing
basis to keep the technology transfer current.[20] Payment is based
on BUMAR's exclusive sales agreements with other Eastern European
countries, nonexclusive sales agreements to certain countries with
which Poland has bilateral clearing agreements, and sales to subsidiaries and affiliates of International Harvester in other areas of
the world. Royalties are paid on each International Harvester machine
sold by BUMAR, with a ceiling beyond which annual royalty payments
may not go. International Harvester committed itself to purchase
machinery produced under license up to an amount twice the value of
the license fee, with rights to purchase more.

The cooperation agreement, which was signed in 1972, is expected to extend until 1990. A reason for the agreement was that
Poland needed the technology that International Harvester was in a
position to provide. It would also enable the Poles to earn hard currency in Western markets and give them a competitive advantage
within the Council for Mutual Economic Assistance (CMEA) market.
Poland was also able to obtain Western sources of financing.[21] International Harvester wanted to gain access to new markets that offered production possibilities, particularly the CMEA market and the
markets of the Third World. It also wanted to expand its product line
by sharing the costs of development and production with BUMAR. For
some products the existing market was not large enough to justify independent development and entry. BUMAR was a large entity in its
own right and had established contacts for its products in much of the
world. Thus, the addition of BUMAR as a partner increased the potential for market penetration and enabled International Harvester to
limit the capital costs of development and production. Finally, lower
labor and supply costs in Poland would work to the advantage of International Harvester in its operations in Western Europe.

The agreement was subsequently broadened to include a British
subsidiary of International Harvester. Demand for new types of
tractors had developed in the United Kingdom, but the construction
of a new plant would have cost millions of dollars and would have duplicated tractors already manufactured at BUMAR's Wola plant in
Stalowa, Poland. The British subsidiary contracted with Stalowa
Wola to purchase tractors without engines, import the latter from
the United States, assemble the tractors in Britain, and sell machines
identical to those made in Chicago, the home base of International
Harvester, and Stalowa Wola.[22] Cooperation between International
Harvester and Stalowa Wola was also extended to the production of

pipeline-laying machines—a special type of tractor for which there is considerable demand in Poland, as well as in other Eastern European countries. An example is the construction of the Orenburg pipeline in the Soviet Union. International Harvester is designing the tractor and Stalowa Wola the pipeline-laying arrangement. Another agreement between International Harvester and BUMAR, which was signed in 1978, provided for another joint-development project to produce torque converters, a hydrokinetic drive for heavy-construction equipment. Continuous negotiations characterize the International Harvester-BUMAR agreement.

A basic problem in East-West trade, which varies from country to country, is quality defects in Eastern-manufactured goods. At first problems of quality developed because the Poles had no particular expertise with quality control standards. Testing procedures generally lagged far behind those employed by Western firms. However, BUMAR was able to solve the problem of its products not meeting U.S. standards, because testing procedures were introduced by International Harvester into BUMAR's plant operations. BUMAR-produced machines carrying the International Harvester label had to satisfy the International Harvester trademark in a qualifying process that involved the testing of parts, first, at the Polish plant and, second, at International Harvester's testing facilities in Phoenix, Arizona, where testing of machinery can last as long as 1,000 hours. However, products carrying the BUMAR label did not have to submit to the same testing and certification procedures as did the International Harvester-labeled products. This has not created a problem in BUMAR's manufacturing process, and engineering design is considered quite good by Western standards. Some production problems, however, have developed in such areas as materials handling, scheduling, and coordination of activities. [23]

Norton-METALEXPORT Agreement

In 1974 the Norton Company of Worcester, Massachusetts, entered into an agreement with the Polish foreign-trade organization METALEXPORT to construct a grinding wheel facility in Kolo, Poland. [24] The Norton Company is the world's largest manufacturer of abrasives. The project called for the provision of manufacturing technology, engineering services, and machinery and equipment to operate the plant. Under the agreement Korund, a Polish state enterprise in Kolo, and part of a combine of enterprises named Ponar-Jotex, assumed responsibility for the operation of the new plant. The 480,000-square-foot facility is Poland's largest grinding wheel plant and one of the most modern of its type in the world. The contract was for $20 million, and a buy-back agreement was involved, which was to continue at least until the end of 1979. Essentially,

Norton has control over all exports from the Polish plant into the hard-currency countries and markets the product line through its own network of sales-marketing organizations called Norton International. Norton has agreed to take a specific yearly volume of the product, grinding wheels, which are used in a broad range of industries for stock removal and finishing of various materials, particularly metals.

Norton has also sold technology for some of its processes involving grinding wheels and coated abrasives to Romania and the Soviet Union. Grinding wheels and coated abrasives are essentially expendable tools in woodworking and metalworking operations from basic steel-mill-rolling processes to precision grinding for production of automotive and aircraft engines and parts. Additionally, one special product, called pulpstones, was involved in the Soviet agreement. It is used in mechanical pulping operations for the production of paper. In the Soviet Union Norton was responsible for the construction of a pulpstone-manufacturing plant in Sverdlovsk. Norton also provided technology, machinery, and equipment under a separate contract. There was no buy-back arrangement—only a cash deal. Norton also entered into an agreement with the Soviet Union that provided for the construction of a plant to produce coated abrasive products such as sandpaper. No royalties were involved in the arrangement, nor were there any buy-back agreements. The total cost of the project came to around $10 million, of which 20 percent went to Norton.

A. Epstein & Sons International

In 1971 the A. Epstein Companies of Chicago concluded the first turnkey contract (worth $8 million) ever signed between a U.S. firm and Poland.[25] It involved the construction of two freezer storage buildings, one at Lublin and one at Lagisza. The Lublin building included an additional area for vegetable processing. The Lagisza building is about 11,000 square meters, and the Lublin building is about 14,000 square meters. The completion of this project was followed by another turnkey contract amounting to $102 million for the construction of three slaughter and meat-packing plants, each of which is about 50,000 square meters. They are located at Ostroda, Sokolow-Podlaski, and Rawa Mazowiecka and are essentially identical except for site adaptation. They are complete meat-processing plants, with hogs and cattle walking on the hoof into the pens on one end and coming out the other end as canned ham, sliced bacon, and other products. The plants include all of the by-products processing such as rendering bones for gelatin processing, casings for sausages, blood separation, and the curing of hides. These plants were started in 1973 and finished in 1975. Each plant produces 60,000 metric tons of finished meat products annually. The slaughtering rates for each plant are 240 hogs per hour, 50 cattle per hour, and 40 smaller animals per hour.

The turnkey projects involved the design, supply, and erection of the buildings; the selection, purchase, and installation of all process equipment;[26] the training of Polish personnel in the United States and Western Europe; the start-up and running-in of the plants to full capacity; U.S. Department of Agriculture approval; and full compliance with specified quality standards. At the peak of the projects, more than 2,000 persons, including 300 Western technicians, were employed. Complete living accommodations—barracks, mess halls, and laundries—were provided for 1,200 persons. Trucks and construction equipment worth more than $1.5 million were used and were a contributing factor to the local economies. Both of the projects were financed by the U.S. Eximbank. The Poles planned to help pay for the plants through exporting some of the products they produced. They also hoped to increase the meat supply in Poland, which has been meager. Their plans have not worked out very well, however, because the export market has shrunk, and their supply of animals has been insufficient to make full use of the plants.[27]

THE FUTURE POTENTIAL FOR
INDUSTRIAL COOPERATION

In the past the economies of Eastern Europe have shown rapid, if uneven, patterns of economic growth. Targets set down in the 1976-80 five-year plans call for a slower growth rate than at any time in the past two decades. Inflationary pressures at home and abroad, higher prices for raw materials, disastrous agricultural harvests, and labor and capital shortages have combined with a psychological reaction against an expansionary economic policy of the first half of this decade and the resulting increase in international debt to produce austerity programs aimed at establishing equilibrium. The goals of the current five-year plans can be reached only by restricting domestic consumption because of the necessity of keeping the growth of imports at about half that of exports. The emphasis on achieving economic equilibrium is reflected in investments, which are being cut back in relation to the 1970-75 plans, partially because of insufficient processing capacity and a lack of labor reserves. The worsening terms of trade of most Eastern European countries, the generally poor prospects for expanding exports to the West, and decisions to sharply curtail imports to reduce the trade deficit and the level of debt are major factors in reducing the Eastern European planned rate of economic growth in the 1976-80 plan period.

Poland's Economic Problems

The leaders of Poland continue to face several major economic problems. One such problem involves satisfying consumer demand. There has been a high level of consumer unrest, which can be attributed to chronic shortages of meat and quality consumer goods. To some extent bad weather contributed to poor agricultural harvests. In 1975 the production of grain was 4 million metric tons less than it was in 1974. The production of potatoes, one of the basic staples of the Polish diet, declined from 50 million metric tons in 1976 to 41 million metric tons in 1977. Meat consumption is also a critical element of the Polish diet. A shortfall in the potato crop—a major source of feed for hogs—forced farmers to purchase livestock feed from the state. This resulted in an increase in Polish grain imports, which impacted heavily on the existing trade deficit. The cost of the grain imports was passed on to the farmers, but it was not matched by higher purchase prices for livestock. Many farmers gave up hog raising. Hog production began to decrease from a high of 21.5 million head in 1974 to 18.8 million head in 1976. The government was forced to initiate stopgap measures to increase domestic supplies of pork. Exports were reduced and imports were increased with few effective results.

Meat shortages have contributed to trade deficits with the West and a hard-currency debt, which was $12.8 billion at the end of 1977. However, agricultural problems are only a part of the total economic picture. To achieve a rapid rate of economic expansion during the early part of the 1970s, Poland imported large amounts of technology from the West, which was paid for with Western credit. The Poles expected to pay off their debt with expanded exports to the West of goods produced by the technology. But the expanded exports failed to materialize, and the hard-currency debt to the West increased (see Table 4). Imports increased faster than Poland's export capabilities, and traditional exports encountered trade barriers and reduced demand in the West. As trade deficits with the West increased, Poland had to increase its rate of borrowing from Western sources. As Western interest rates increased, reflecting the pervasive inflation in the West, interest payments to the West increased rapidly. The debt-service ratio, which is the percentage relationship between the repayment of principal on medium- and long-term debt and interest on all debt to merchandise exports to the West, increased from 20 percent in 1970 to 60 percent in 1977.

The growth of exports to the West has not kept pace with the growth of imports and the increase in the hard-currency debt. As borrowing has increased, Poland has become more and more dependent on private credit from Western commercial banks. In 1970 debt

TABLE 4

Poland: Exports, Imports, Outstanding Net Debt, and Debt-Service
Ratios, 1970-77
(millions of dollars)

Year	Merchandise Exports	Merchandise Imports	Net Debt	Debt-Service Ratio
1970	962	901	770	20
1971	1,099	1,075	800	19
1972	1,397	1,772	1,100	20
1973	2,063	3,431	1,900	21
1974	2,865	5,233	3,950	27
1975	3,026	6,076	6,930	43
1976	3,373	6,636	10,200	49
1977	3,660	6,120	12,800	60

Source: U.S., Central Intelligence Agency, National Foreign
Assessment Center, "The Scope of Poland's Economic Dilemma,"
mimeographed (Washington, D.C.: CIA, July 1978), p. 7.

to Western commercial banks amounted to $80 million; by 1977 the
amount of debt owed to Western commercial banks had increased to
$7.4 billion, or 60 percent of the net debt.[28] The increase in debt-
service payments, which resulted from a rising debt, forced Poland
to seek easier credit terms in the West and to appeal to the Soviet
Union for financial assistance. This took the form of R1 billion loan,
shipments of grain and crude oil, and provision of certain consumer
goods. But this assistance, by itself, is not sufficient to solve Poland's balance-of-payments problems, which are expected to extend
into the 1980s. It is conceivable that by 1980 debt-service payments
could consume as much as 80 percent of export earnings. Poland
would then be faced with the alternative of either having to obtain additional credit from the West or reducing the volume of its imports.
  Nevertheless, there is the need on the part of the authorities
to respond to increasing consumer unrest. The 1976-80 economic
plan had to be revised to placate consumers, with increased priority
attached to an increase in investments in the food, housing, and commercial service areas. An important aspect of the revised plan is
the placing of more reliance on the Polish economy's private sector

to stimulate an increase in the output of consumer goods and services. Many concessions have been made to private enterprises, including reducing taxes on private businesses and raising the tax-free limit on private service income by 500 percent. Credit has been increased to private enterprises, private artisans and craftsmen have been included in the social security system, and local government offices have been created to help private artisans obtain commercial facilities and supplies of materials and equipment. Foreign investment, particularly by Poles domiciled abroad, in private Polish business ventures has been encouraged. As mentioned previously, recent decrees of the Council of Ministers are designed to attract foreign investment into consumer goods and service areas, with special financial concessions offered to attract the foreign investor.

One key to the solution of Poland's hard-currency-debt problems is to increase export earnings. Coal is an important factor in export earnings, providing about $1 billion annually in hard-currency earnings. But there are restraints placed on exports of coal by rising domestic needs and an inadequate production capacity. Moreover, the modernization of Polish industry with technology imported from the West has failed to enhance the growth of Polish exports to its hard-currency creditors. One example is the performance of the Polish automotive industry, which was developed to a major degree through industrial cooperation with the French, in which the latter provided equipment, technology, and licenses. Exports of automobiles, buses, and trucks have not provided the desired hard currency, at least in part because automotive parts continue to be imported from the West. However, this problem may be short-lived, for some payoff is expected from cooperation agreements that provide for exports of Polish trucks in the early 1980s. The same holds true for other industrial-cooperation agreements, with the production of Ursus tractors under a U.K. licensing agreement not scheduled for export until late 1978 and production of other products under licensing agreements scheduled for 1979 and 1980.

The Future of Industrial-Cooperation
Agreements with Poland

The potential for U.S. business involvement in industrial-cooperation agreements appears to be mixed. If Poland cannot secure sufficient aid with respect to its hard-currency debt, it will have to make further cutbacks in imports and economic growth. Of course, any agreement that would provide an opportunity to earn hard currency would at least receive some favorable consideration. But there are certain problems that tend to inhibit the formation of certain types of agreements. For many products Western markets have become saturated. It is estimated that 50 percent of coproduction agreements involving West German firms and the Eastern European countries, including Poland, have resulted in the production of goods that face saturated Western markets.[29] This tends to confirm the product life cycle model. Moreover, much of the technology available for export is obsolete by Western standards. There is the inability of Polish production to adjust to changes in foreign demand. But probably the most important problem confronting the Poles is a lack of managerial and marketing expertise. Western management expertise, if imparted in an industrial-cooperation agreement, is often lost in the process of assimilation into a different environment.

The Poles have had to scale down their economic aspirations, at least for the immediate future. Key policy decisions made at the onset of the 1970s turned out to be wrong, in part through circumstances over which the Gierek government had no control. Emphasis was placed on modernizing the economy of Poland and improving living standards. Massive imports of Western technology paid for with readily available Western credit were supposed to provide the capital infusion necessary for the modernization of the economy. But the economic recession in the West, which began in 1973, created export problems and reduced opportunities to earn hard currency. Polish retrenchment with respect to imports did not occur, because the Poles believed that domestic political stability was linked to continued improvements in living standards—improvements that could only be attained through the importation of technology from the West. All of this has changed with the revised 1976-80 national economic plan, and thus the future involvement of U.S. firms in business ventures with Poland appears to be somewhat limited.

A negative trade balance has existed between Poland and the United States over the last six years, exacerbating Poland's hard-currency and balance-of-payments problems (see Table 5). There is a need to improve the access of Polish exports to the U.S. market. Even though Poland enjoys most-favored-nation (MFN) status with the United States, U.S. protectionist policies are of concern to Polish foreign-trade organizations and state enterprises. One example is the application of the Trade Act of 1974 to the alleged dumping of Polish Melex golf carts in the United States. The requirement of establishing the relevant fair value based on the price of a similar product sold by a U.S. manufacturer could deprive Polish exporters of the possibility of creating effective competition in the United States, thus losing part of the U.S. market and increasing the balance-of-payments problem. There are also other problems in U.S.-Polish trade, particularly import quotas, which currently concern such products as textile articles and steel rods, and licensing procedures and other forms of tariff and nontariff protectionism.

TABLE 5

Polish-U.S. Trade and Trade Balance, 1972-78
(current prices in millions of dollars)

Year	Total	Exports	Imports	Trade Balance
1972	263.4	141.7	121.7	20.0
1973	504.6	190.1	314.5	-124.4
1974	732.8	259.3	473.5	-214.2
1975	823.6	234.1	589.5	-355.4
1976	1,114.3	282.0	832.3	-550.3
1977	910.8	365.5	545.3	-179.8
1978*	703.0	304.6	398.4	-93.8

*Preliminary statistics.

Source: Research Institute of Foreign Trade, Warsaw, Poland, unpublished paper, December 1978.

A report by the Brookings Institution provided a rather pessimistic appraisal of trade potential between East and West for the remainder of the 1970s.[30] The appraisal was based on Eastern European indebtedness to the West at the end of 1977 and the ratio of debt-service costs to exports. A ratio in excess of 0.25 is considered by international bankers to be a cause for concern. The ratios for the Eastern European countries range from 0.28 for the Soviet Union to 0.85 for Bulgaria. The ratio for Poland is 0.60, second only to Bulgaria and well above the ratio of 0.20 for 84 developing countries.[31] The Polish ratio of net debt to exports in 1976 was 2.5 to 1.0 compared with an average of 1.1 to 1.0 for all Eastern European countries. At first glance it would appear that Poland is a poor credit risk, but it has the power to attempt to correct external imbalances by imposing austerity measures at home at the expense of consumers. However, there are apparent limits to which consumers can be squeezed, as witnessed by the riots in 1975 when there was an attempt to raise food prices. Eastern European consumers are becoming a powerful force—subsidies paid to keep consumer prices stable testify to this. Increases in exports or decreases in imports call for sacrifices to be made either in personal consumption or in investments in such areas as housing.

Reduction in Imports

The current Polish five-year plan calls for a reduction in imports compared with the prior plan. This solution, however, can at best serve as a temporary palliative for the debt problem. It conserves hard currency in the short run but does not provide any long-run solution to the imbalance in trade that causes the debt problem. The reduction in imports can also slow the pace of industrialization necessary to increase living standards. The whole planning process is diverted as it becomes necessary to find substitutes for imports needed to fulfill plan objectives. A chain reaction can set in, creating shortfalls in target plans that have to be filled. Although it is true that certain unnecessary imports can be eliminated, Poland may find that it cannot do without essential imports vital to industrial growth. Industrial development in Poland and other Eastern European countries has created an interdependence with Western technology.

Increase in Exports

A second approach to reducing hard-currency indebtedness to the West is to increase the volume of exports. This is easier said than done. Poland has failed to increase exports at the current plan rate of 5 percent per year. There has been a slow recovery from the Western economic recession, with an attendant sluggish demand for imports by the West. However, the cyclic fluctuations in the West account for only a small fraction of the lower export performance. Poland and the other Eastern European countries also have to confront a trend toward increased protectionism in many Western countries. Eastern exports to Western markets encounter a very competitive environment in which not only considerations of product quality are important but also the need for extensive marketing skills and support in the form of services. In fact receiving MFN treatment does not automatically guarantee success for Polish exports, for the Poles are deficient in support services. Finally, structural problems in the Polish economy limit the amount of exports available for Western markets.

Countertrade

A third approach to dealing with hard-currency constraints is increasing Polish reliance on various forms of countertrade, particularly the counterpurchase agreement. In terms of the volume of trade generated through countertrade, Poland ranks second only to the Soviet Union as a socialist participant. Poland's interest in countertrade has increased along with its debt to the West, and countertrade is expected to reach at least 50 percent of export contract value by 1980.[32] Polish countertrade demand is greatest for sales of Western plants, technology, and equipment for the electronics and heavy-equipment industries. Nearly all Polish purchases of Western electronics equipment require the purchase of goods equal to 10 to 50 percent of the contract value. Countertrade is commonly used in major projects involving Polish and foreign investment, with no equity participation by foreign firms. An example is the Massey-Ferguson contract with Poland, valued at $350 million, in which the Poles agreed to purchase equipment for the Ursus tractor plant; in return Massey-Ferguson agreed to buy back Polish diesel engines and tractors.[33] Countertrade is also used in natural resource development projects in which the Poles agree to exchange coal or other raw materials in return for the purchase of Western equipment to be used in the projects.

A trade policy based on countertrade creates several problems for Poland. First, it limits options available to Polish foreign-trade organizations and state enterprises in the future with respect to marketing decisions, including the important questions of the markets they may wish to serve and the prices they can charge in the future. Second, countertrade does not solve the fundamental marketing problems associated with Polish goods. Rather, this policy passes responsibility for marketing to someone else—namely, a Western partner. The Western partner may have the marketing expertise to fulfill the task efficiently, but the long-run effect for the Polish partner is minimal. Third, countertrade can contribute little to the development of technology-intensive industries. Finally, an important factor that can impinge upon countertrade is a developing energy shortage. The Soviet Union is the paramount source of oil for Poland, and it is raising prices while failing to meet production targets. Poland is facing a shortfall in oil and must draw upon alternative energy sources to satisfy domestic needs. There are capacity constraints, as domestic demand is increasing and industrial production is behind schedule.

Poland is set for a period of consolidation aimed at attaining a greater balance in foreign trade and a leveling off in growth rates to allow for the restructuring of certain industrial sectors. The 1978 plan sought to ease the immediate pressure of consumer demand by increasing the output of consumer goods, but at considerable cost to industrial growth. The plan called for an all-out effort to boost exports and limit imports and placed priority on the development of agriculture, food processing, housing construction, and the expansion of services.[34] A tenuous modus vivendi between the state and the Roman Catholic church appears to be strengthened with the election of a Polish bishop as pope—Pope John Paul II. For the present a state of euphoria exists among most Poles, but this could be short-lived if the economy deteriorates or the government announces price increases on basic goods. The severe winter of 1978/79 exacerbated Poland's fuel and energy balance. With the exception of Romania, which is self-sufficient in oil, Poland and the other Eastern European countries must depend on the Soviet Union for the bulk of their crude oil; however, the Soviets have indicated a preference for selling any surplus oil to the West in exchange for hard currency.

The economic problems of Poland do not automatically rule out further industrial-cooperation agreements with the West. In recent years a number of measures have been taken in Poland to encourage commercial and industrial enterprises to strengthen cooperative ties with other countries. The decision-making process involved in industrial cooperation has been simplified, and investments necessary for a proper organization of cooperative deliveries have been facilitated. Foreign investment, although limited to certain types of activities, is permitted in Poland and is particularly desirable when the end result is to attract hard currency. The current five-year plan calls for an increase in exports and also places a priority on stimulating certain sectors of the Polish economy—agriculture, food processing, and services. Therefore, it is incumbent upon U.S. firms interested in cooperation agreements with Poland to be aware of priorities established in the plan. Any project that will conserve or earn hard currency is desirable. In fact, an executive of John Deere sees no deterrents in conducting future business with Poland and other Eastern European countries and expresses the opinion that cooperation agreements are the only way to do business in those countries that are so desperately short of hard currency.

SUMMARY

Poland's industrial cooperation with capitalist enterprises began in the early 1960s. Most of the initial cooperation agreements were with Western European countries, particularly France and Italy. As relations improved with West Germany, industrial enterprises from that country became active in concluding agreements with Poland. U.S. participation in cooperation agreements with Poland came late, despite a natural affinity between the two countries and the fact that Poland was the first Eastern European country to be granted MFN status. U.S. business involvement in Poland developed in the early 1970s and was expedited by the expansionary economic plan of the Gierek regime. Polish laws have made it relatively easy to conclude cooperation agreements, for Polish state enterprises have had the authority to conclude these agreements for some time. The existence of these laws is already an advantage to the U.S. negotiator; the substantive provisions bear the imprimatur of the Council of Ministers. State enterprises may enter into cooperation agreements when the arrangement is in the interest of the export trade, the domestic market, or the reduction of imports.

By the middle 1970s Poland began to develop a set of economic problems that stemmed in part from policies initiated in the 1970-75 plan that were designed concomitantly to accomplish rapid industrialization and to raise living standards. Much technology was imported from the West, with credit made readily available by Western sources. But Polish exports could not keep pace with an increase in the Polish debt to the West and increases in imports to satisfy consumer demand. Problems developed at home, including meat shortages and poor agricultural harvests. The 1976-80 plan scaled down Polish expectations, but it had to be revised as debt payments to the West mushroomed. Imports, which had been projected to increase at an average annual rate of 9.4 percent in the original version of the plan, were reduced to an annual rate of 4.7 percent. Exports were also scaled down from an annual increase of 15.6 percent to 11.8 percent. Debt rescheduling and new sources of financial assistance can provide a palliative for Poland's problems in the short run, but these problems could be exacerbated if cutbacks in Soviet oil deliveries occur as is anticipated. But all of this does not rule out continued industrial cooperation between Poland and U.S. firms.

NOTES

1. In Poland approximately 85 percent of all agricultural land is privately owned. Private enterprise is permitted in many consumer-service areas. Private employers may employ up to five workers.

2. Jan Grabowski and Eugeniusz Tabaczynski, "East-West International Investment and Production Ventures," Handel Jagraniczny 19 (1974): 8-14.

3. U.S., Congress, Joint Economic Committee in "East-West Industrial Cooperation," prepared by Carl H. McMillan, 95th Cong., 1st sess., August 25, 1977, p. 1209. The Soviet Union is not included.

4. Henry Z. Horbaczewski, "Profitable Coexistence: The Legal Foundation for Joint Enterprises with U.S. Participation in Poland," Business Lawyer 31 (November 1975): 446-48.

5. Ibid., p. 447.

6. Council of Ministers Decree no. 123, May 14, 1976.

7. Ibid., par. 10.

8. Ministry of Finance Decree no. 109, June 14, 1976, par. 3.

9. Robert S. Kretschmar and Robin Foor, The Potential for Joint Ventures in Eastern Europe (New York: Praeger, 1972), p. 70.

10. International Development Research Center, "Technology Transfer: Statistical Findings and Analysis" (chap. 4) (Study prepared for the Bureau of East-West Trade, U.S. Department of Commerce, Indiana University, October 1975), table 2, p. 6 and chart 1, p. 7.

11. Ibid., p. 5 and table 2.

12. Ibid., table 2, p. 6.

13. Ibid., table 3, pp. 11, 13.

14. The data on the RCA-Corning and UNITRA agreement were provided by Farnham Shaw, project director for the Corning share of the project.

15. The data on the Grace-WEGLOKOKS agreement is based on Agency Agreement 2A, March 1, 1973.

16. Ibid., p. 2.

17. Ibid., pp. 2-5.

18. In 1977 International Harvester was the twenty-eighth largest U.S. corporation and the thirteenth largest industrial exporter.

19. BUMAR Union is under the jurisdiction of the Ministry of Machine Industry. BUMAR Union can be considered as a form of trust that has control over the operations of enterprises in a given economic field.

20. For a more comprehensive discussion of the International Harvester-BUMAR agreement, see "Industrial Cooperation between International Harvester and BUMAR in the Production of Construction Machinery," working draft of a case study carried out as a part of a research project on U.S.-Polish industrial cooperation, carried out by an Indiana University-based team in collaboration with the Foreign Trade Research Institute of Poland's Ministry of Foreign Trade and Shipping. Cited with permission.

21. Initially, a $2.7 million credit from Eximbank at 7 percent covered 45 percent of the value of tractors and components supplied to BUMAR. Another 45 percent was provided by private sources and guaranteed by Eximbank, and the remaining 10 percent came from a Polish bank.

22. Information provided by International Harvester at the request of the author.

23. Working draft of the International Harvester-BUMAR agreement.

24. Data provided by the Norton Company.

25. Data provided by A. Epstein Companies.

26. Machinery for the plants was purchased from Western European firms.

27. A number of problems were associated with the construction of these plants. One plant was destroyed by fire before it began op-

erations. Polish engineers, although well trained in theoretical matters, lacked practical experience. There were problems of recruiting workers, and Polish engineers were unwilling to make decisions on questions as they arose in daily operations.

28. U.S., Central Intelligence Agency, National Foreign Assessment Center, "The Scope of Poland's Economic Dilemma," mimeographed (Washington, D.C.: CIA, July 1978), pp. 1-15.

29. Ibid., p. 8.

30. Brookings Institution, Economic Relations between East and West: Prospects and Problems (Washington, D.C.: Brookings Institution, July 1978).

31. Ibid., p. 23.

32. Edwin Zagorski, "U.S.-Polish Industrial Cooperation: Achievements, Problems, Prospects" (Paper presented at a symposium on U.S.-Poland trade relations, University of Indiana, December 1978).

33. Data provided by the Massey-Ferguson Company.

34. Zagorski, "U.S.-Polish Industrial Cooperation," pp. 12-13.

5
INDUSTRIAL COOPERATION
IN HUNGARY

A series of economic reforms, the most important of which took place in 1968, has been a distinctive feature of the Hungarian economy. These reforms were designed to promote administrative and economic efficiency. In 1968 enterprises were made independent economic units with the right to determine the structure of their production and sales. This policy conformed to one basic objective of the reform—namely, to relieve the planning authorities of the task of preparing intricate economic plans. Instead, broad guidelines were provided for enterprises to follow. Enterprises were given latitude with respect to quality, styling, and pricing. They were also given the right to determine their own production mix on the basis of their preferences. A modified market economy was permitted in which enterprises could react to consumer preferences. Nevertheless, the central planning authorities were able to exercise some control over enterprise production through the use of economic levers designed to induce cooperation by making it more profitable to produce certain items. Thus, the government reserved the final right to curb consumer preferences, particularly in the public area. Moreover, all major macroeconomic decisions concerning economic development, living standards, and investment and consumption remained in the hands of the state.

The Soviet rapprochement with the United States significantly loosened the constraint that Hungary had felt on its own economic relations with the West. However, the structure of Hungarian foreign trade was unsatisfactory—its machinery was of poor quality, acceptable only to other Eastern European countries, and trade with the West was mainly an exchange of agricultural goods for raw materials. Hungary could not import enough advanced Western technology, nor could competition from imports be used to prod domestic producers

into improving quality. It was deemed necessary to encourage an infusion of Western technology, management, and capital. Beginning
around 1965, Hungary became quite active in concluding industrial-
cooperation agreements with Western firms. The special attraction
of these agreements stemmed from the possibilities that they offered
as instruments through which several external economic policy objectives could be pursued concomitantly: an increase in trade with
the West, a more desirable trade structure through an increase in
manufacturing exports to the West, and a more effective acquisition
and absorption of Western technology. Industrial-cooperation agreements with the West also offered the prospect of reducing the adverse
balance-of-payments effect of increased acquisition of Western capital goods and technology.

LEGAL FRAMEWORK FOR
INDUSTRIAL COOPERATION

Effects of the 1968 Reforms

Hungarian legislation stipulates various forms for foreign firms
to do business within the country. In conformity with the Hungarian
reforms of 1968, manufacturing and trading companies are free to
establish direct contacts with foreign firms, conclude contracts, and
engage in independent foreign-trade activities. The cooperative activities of Hungarian firms are not regulated by special legislation
nor governed by central authority. Coordination of cooperation agreements is done by an interministerial committee subordinate to the
Ministry of Foreign Trade.[1] Conversely, Hungarian statutory provisions impose practically no restrictions on foreign firms wishing
to explore the possibilities of entering the Hungarian market. Representatives of foreign firms may stay in Hungary for a period of up
to six months with a visa issued by the host company. Foreign companies are free to establish direct trade representation in Hungary,
provided it is in the interest of the national economy and foreign-
trade policy. Ties with Western firms are seen as a way to stimulate
greater efficiency and specialization on the part of Hungarian enterprises.

A Ministry of Finance decree of 1972 set forth conditions under
which Western joint-equity ventures with Hungarian partners could be
undertaken. These conditions were quite circumscribed in terms of
the Western partner's operating flexibility.[2] For example, Western
equity interest in a joint venture was limited to a minority share.
This was modified in 1977, when Hungarian legislation made it possible for Western firms to have a majority share in joint-equity ven-

tures. Joint ventures also limited the Western partner to a nonpar-
ticipatory role in production. Thus, participation had to be indirect
in order to conform with socialist restrictions against private ownership of the means of production. For practical purposes joint ventures are limited to nonproducing enterprises such as trading companies and banks. The result is that few joint ventures have been
concluded between Hungarian and Western enterprises. This could
change, as the Hungarians have attempted to relax the restrictions
on joint ventures that prevailed before 1977. The Ministry of Finance
is authorized to allow favorable tax treatment to Western and Hungarian enterprises that engage in joint-venture arrangements.

In March 1978 Hungary was granted most-favored-nation (MFN)
treatment by the United States. Business relations between the United
States and Hungary were improved with the signing of a commercial
agreement. The United States was given the right to open a commercial office in Budapest to balance the existing Hungarian office in New
York. Access by business representatives to each country was eased,
providing greater access for U.S. firms in Hungary. Convertible
currency accounts may be opened by each country, and there are to
be no restrictions on transfers in connection with business transactions. The agreement also modified those provisions of the General
Agreement on Tariffs and Trade (GATT) that deal with market disruptions. The Hungarians agreed that exceptions to MFN treatment
could be made by the United States in cases of "disruption" of U.S.
markets, in accord with the provisions of the U.S. Trade Act. GATT,
on the other hand, requires a finding of serious injury to a domestic
market before a member can alter the MFN status of another country.
Hungary and the United States are both GATT signatories.

Benefits and Disadvantages of Joint Ventures

Certain tax benefits redound to the advantage of Hungarian firms
if joint-venture agreements are entered into with Western firms.[3]
First, Hungarian state enterprises have to pay a tax of 40 percent on
the amount of depreciation. When joint ventures are involved, however, there is no tax on depreciation. Second, Hungarian enterprises
have to pay a capital charge on assets to the government, since the
state is technically the owner of the assets. Joint ventures with Western partners exempt Hungarian enterprises from payment of this
charge. Third, Hungarian state enterprises on the average have to
pay a tax on profits of 70 percent, but joint ventures have to pay only
40 percent if profits are not more than 20 percent of capital stock,
with a maximum profit tax of 60 percent. Fourth, profit taxes are
normally due as soon as an enterprise's balance sheet is drawn up,

but joint ventures can request a return of at least part of the tax if profits are to be reinvested in the venture. Finally, deductions from the profits of a joint venture, if placed in reserve or share funds, are exempt from taxation, whereas the entire profit of a Hungarian enterprise, regardless of its disposal, is subject to the tax.

On an a priori basis, it would appear that there are considerable advantages, at least to a Hungarian enterprise, of entering into a joint venture with a Western partner. However, there can be disadvantages as well as advantages to the Western partner. For example, since Western partners are limited to a maximum of 49 percent ownership in joint ventures, there is a concern that the Hungarian partner will always have the upper hand in terms of voting. But Hungarian law permits the Western partner to specify in the joint-venture contract matters that require a unanimous decision. There is also concern over a proviso in the joint-venture laws that prohibits direct Western involvement in production. But this can be circumvented in that the Western partner, as is true in the case of a holding company, is given complete access to Hungarian production facilities to promote more efficient production. Basically, the Hungarian enterprise is supposed to provide the existing production facilities, while the Western partner is supposed to provide the technical expertise, including sophisticated machinery and know-how, and cash.

Pricing could be a basic problem of any joint-venture agreement. There are actually two pricing problems—fixing the price for the Western markets and fixing the price for the Eastern European markets. In the case of the former, the Hungarian partner can furnish the product at an agreed-upon price, and profit would depend upon the difference between this price and the price at which the product is sold by the Western partner in the world market. This profit would then be divided between the two partners in the venture. However, the pricing system in Eastern Europe is much more difficult, because pricing is often arbitrary and does not reflect costs of production. Often there are many state subsidies that are reflected in such things as raw materials, services, and transportation. There is the problem of incorporating these services as a part of production costs and, thus, charging a price that would yield a profit. There is the need for the Western partner to clarify all price arrangements for goods sold in the Hungarian and Council for Mutual Economic Assistance markets before a joint-venture contract is signed.

Joint ventures may also be inhibited by other factors. One factor of no small importance involves a dissimilar relationship between the economies in which a joint venture has to meld together. In a capitalist economy, an enterprise is free to operate subject to few constraints; in a centrally planned, state-managed economy, an enterprise must function within the framework of bureaucratic constraints imposed by the economic plan. A joint venture, to function success-fully, would have to be given more independence than the typical state enterprise—an independence that a state bureaucracy might be reluc-tant to give. Then, too, a joint venture could demonstrate the supe-riority of Western management techniques to the detriment of the state-managed enterprises. A certain ambivalence exists with re-spect to Eastern European attitudes toward importing Western man-agerial know-how. They, of course, recognize the need to promote efficiency in order to be competitive in international markets, but, on the other hand, the importance of Western management techniques represents a challenge to the status quo. Eastern managers do not have the training or flexibility of their Western counterparts, and they must deal with a bureaucracy, the competency of which is often un-clear. There is often a reluctance to make decisions that could con-ceivably redound to the disadvantage of the Eastern manager.

There is no particular evidence to indicate that joint ventures have opened up a new dimension of cooperation between capitalist and socialist enterprises. In Yugoslavia they have proved to be quite popular, with some 140 concluded between capitalist and Yugoslav enterprises. However, the brand of Yugoslav socialism is entirely different from that which is practiced in the more conventional so-cialist countries of the Comecon (Council for Mutual Economic As-sistance) group. In Hungary and Romania, the two countries that of-ficially permit joint ventures, only a few are in existence. It is nec-essary to remember that the joint-venture laws have only been in ef-fect for a short period of time, and thus it is too early to draw gen-eral conclusions. In Hungary joint-venture agreements in effect with Western firms as of July 1978 involved the following: Volvo, the Swedish car manufacturer formed a joint venture with the Czepel Automobile Works called Volcom to produce cross-country vehicles. Volcom produces two standard models—an open and a closed car—for sale in both Eastern and Western markets. The car is marketed for foreign distribution by the Mogurt Foreign Trade Organization of Hungary. [4]

Two other joint ventures involve the West German electrical equipment producer Siemens and the U.S. firm Corning, which is also active in Poland. The first venture, Sicontact, is between Sie-mens and the Hungarian enterprise Intercooperation to provide tech-nical consulting, after-sales services, and training for all of Sie-mens's electrical products sold in Hungary. [5] The second joint ven-ture is between Corning and the Radelkis Electro-Chemical Instru-ments Cooperative and the Metrimpex Foreign Trade Organization. The joint venture, called Radelcor, produces blood gas analyzers. [6] In this venture Corning provides technology and certain components, while Radelkis provides the production facilities. Corning is responsible for the distribution and sales of the blood gas analyzers in Western Europe, and Metrimpex has the same responsibility in Eastern Europe. Corning discontinued production of the analyzers at its subsidiary in the United Kingdom, citing as reasons lower costs of production in Hungary and an increased ability to penetrate the Eastern European market through the use of Hungarian outlets.

Dow Chemical Corporation has had discussions with Poland, Hungary, and Romania concerning possible joint ventures.[7] Its experience with joint ventures in Yugoslavia has proved to be successful. Total investment by Dow in Yugoslavia is projected to be close to $1 billion, and total sales in Eastern Europe amount to around $200 million. It has concluded protocols with Eastern European countries involving five-year periods during which both parties have expressed an intent to buy and sell specified products, aiming at stated dollar figures of annual trade value. As for joint ventures, Dow finds the Hungarian and Romanian systems and foreign investment laws flexible enough to allow the foreign partner to achieve a share of profits commensurate with its investment, but so far no joint ventures have been concluded with either country. In the case of Poland, joint-venture rules are such—with regard to control of the enterprise, availability of foreign exchange, and the means whereby the foreign partner can receive its share of the monetary benefits—that Dow has not been able to reconcile them with its criteria for a profitable venture.

Joint ventures are by no means limited to Hungarian soil. A law passed in 1975 permits Hungarian enterprises to enter into joint ventures in third countries for the purpose of promoting production services and foreign marketing activities. In fact Hungarian foreign-trade organizations and state enterprises have entered into joint ventures with Western firms to produce and distribute products in Western Europe and the United States. In 1978 the Hungarian state enterprise United Incandescent Lamp & Electrical Company (Tungsram) entered into an agreement with Action Industries of Cheswick, Pennsylvania, to manufacture light bulbs at a new factory at East Brunswick, New Jersey.[8] The joint venture, called Action Tungsram, will also import about 60 million household bulbs from Tungsram to supplement its U.S. production and will import industrial-lighting products including quartz, halogens, mercury, xenon, and fluorescent lamps. It will also import Hungarian bulb-making machinery for sale in U.S. markets. The financing arrangement of the venture involved a $1.3 million capital contribution from Tungsram, $2.1 million in loan guarantees from the State Bank of Hungary, and a loan guarantee from the Union National Bank of Pittsburgh. Action Industries has a 51 percent stock holding, and Tungsram holds 49 percent.

HUNGARIAN INDUSTRIAL-COOPERATION
AGREEMENTS

Industrial-cooperation agreements, as opposed to joint ventures, are far more numerous in Hungary. As of 1978 Hungary had some 400 industrial-cooperation agreements with the West and is interested in promoting still more. To encourage industrial cooperation, the Hungarian government is prepared to grant a variety of concessions to Western firms. Tax concessions, including accelerated amortization of capital investment and waiver of taxes when products are exported abroad, are offered to the Hungarian and Western partners in a cooperation agreement. Import licenses, normally required for products imported from the West into Hungary, are given on a preferential basis to the cooperative partners along with an assurance of convertible currency. The Hungarian partner in an industrial-cooperation agreement is also given preferential treatment with respect to the allocation of credit from funds available to promote Hungarian exports, at lower interest rates and with a longer repayment period. And there are benefits accruing from the full or partial refunding of tariffs. Other concessions to industrial cooperation include more lenient requirements involving counterpurchase agreements and the use of running license fees on Western technology instead of lump-sum payments, which are customarily used in other Eastern European countries.

The great majority of industrial-cooperation agreements are concluded with Western European firms, particularly those from Austria and West Germany. At least half of these agreements involve licensing of patents, copyrights, and production know-how, with provision for partial payment of fees in the form of output. Examples of cooperation agreements are presented in the following paragraph.

The West German firm Badische-Anilin (BASF) entered into an agreement with the Polimer Cooperative to manufacture recording tape. BASF supplies machinery and raw materials, and the product is marketed in both Hungary and West Germany. Mannesmann of West Germany and the Hungarian GANZ Electric Works signed a co-operative agreement to build a power plant in Greece, with the West German firm providing the turbines and GANZ the generators.[9] The Hungarian Komplex Trading Company entered into a cooperative agreement with the Austrian firm VEW to deliver a turnkey plant to Iraq that will extract liquid sugar from dates. Glass, a West German firm, and Komplex jointly market farm equipment in South America. The Swedish Saab-Scania Company, producers of motor vehicles, and the Hungarian Mogurt Foreign Trade Organization jointly own a company in Iraq that produces Hungarian Ikarus buses.

U.S. Industrial-Cooperation Agreements

Tabulated cooperative agreements of all types completed or in force between U.S. and Hungarian enterprises totaled 35 at the end of 1975. A number of other agreements have been concluded since that time.[10] Around half of the agreements were licensing agreements, with most of the remainder being coproduction and turnkey agreements. Most of the licensing agreements involved payment in products. The majority of U.S.-Hungarian cooperation agreements tend to be small in scale and entail the processing of intermediate products. An exception is an agreement between the Steiger Tractor Company and the Hungarian Railway Carriage and Machine Works (RABA), which involves $100 million in trade over a five-year period. In Hungary there does not appear to be the clear dominance of industrial cooperation by the giant U.S. multinationals. Of the 35 cooperation agreements referred to above, 23 were concluded by firms listed in Fortune's 500 select list compared with 62 out of 74 agreements concluded in Poland for the same period.[11] The most active industrial sectors in the use of cooperation agreements with U.S. firms are the Hungarian mechanical engineering and machine tool industries.

Philip Morris

Philip Morris is a multinational corporation in the true sense of the word, deriving more than 40 percent of its total revenue from foreign operations. In 1978 Philip Morris sold 168 billion units of cirgarettes in the United States compared with 201 billion units sold abroad. It sells over 160 brands in more than 170 countries through 25 manufacturing and marketing affiliates, 38 licensees, and regional export sales organizations. In 1978 the Swiss subsidiary of Philip Morris, Fabriques de Tabac Réunies, acquired the Liggett Group. This acquisition gave Philip Morris the rights to existing Liggett trademarks outside the United States, as well as related rights, patents, and technical data. Liggett international brands covered by the purchase included Lark, L & M, Chesterfield, Eve, and Decade. In a related transaction Philip Morris bought international inventories, receivables, and other assets from the Liggett Group. Moreover, the Philip Morris brand Marlboro continues to be the world's best-selling cirgarette, accounting for more than one-third of the company's international sales. In some countries Marlboro is the only Philip Morris cigarette licensed to be sold, because the recognition factor is so great. This is of particular importance in the Eastern European countries, where advertising know-how is rudimentary at best.

Philip Morris was the first U.S. cigarette company to diversify into other activities and to expand its operations overseas—both in response to recurring adverse health reports in the United States.

In 1978 its domestic sales of cigarettes were 168 billion units out of total industry sales of 601 billion units. [12] Its increase in sales over 1977 amounted to 5.3 percent compared with an increase of 1.7 percent for the cigarette industry as a whole. The world's cigarette market excluding the United States was 3.6 trillion units for 1978, an increase of 2.7 percent over 1977. Philip Morris's share of this market was 201 million units in 1978, for an increase of 7.8 percent over 1977. On both a domestic and an international basis, the company has outperformed the industry. However, consumption of cigarettes in Western Europe is leveling off as countries have imposed restrictions on cigarette advertising on television and in the newspapers. Heavy taxes have also been imposed on the sale of cigarettes. So it has become desirable for Philip Morris and other cigarette companies to seek new markets for cigarettes and related tobacco products.

One such market is Eastern Europe. There are several factors that favor expansion into this market. First of all, the level of cigarette consumption in Eastern Europe is high and can be expected to increase in the future. [13] In Poland, for example, it is estimated that 60 percent of all adult males and 65 percent of all adult females smoke. Second, there are no general proscriptions against cigarette smoking as there are in the United States and Western Europe. Third, the level of disposable income is higher than in such markets as Africa and Asia. Finally, the production and sale of cigarettes in the Eastern European markets entails little drain on hard-currency reserves. Since there is a general shortage of most consumer goods, but particularly cars, there are not many items on which money can be spent. Cigarettes constitute such an item, and they also provide an excellent source of revenue to the state. Therefore, the Eastern European market and now the market of the People's Republic of China constitute areas of growth for cigarette consumption. In China alone there are an estimated 400 million smokers—a large market that Philip Morris intends to develop.

Philip Morris has licensing agreements with almost all of the Eastern European countries, including Hungary and Poland, to produce the Marlboro cigarette. There is a prestige factor attached to smoking the Marlboro cigarette, even though it costs more than competing socialist cigarettes. Marlboros are manufactured in Hungary, subject to quality control standards set by Philip Morris. Samples of the cigarettes are sent to the company's manufacturing center in Richmond, Virginia, to ensure that they follow quality control standards. The Marlboro cigarette is standardized worldwide. Philip Morris also supplies technical and marketing information and sells the Hungarians burley tobacco from Kentucky and Tennessee. The Hungarians pay for this tobacco in hard currency. Royalties are also paid to Philip Morris based on the number of cigarettes produced and sold. Philip Morris generally tries to avoid countertrade agreements, but it does not rule them out. Countertrade agreements have been in effect in which burley tobacco has been exchanged for Turkish tobacco produced in the Soviet Union. Philip Morris rates the potential for continued business in Hungary and the rest of Eastern Europe as quite good, with growth rates in the consumption of cigarettes much higher than in Western Europe.

Hesston-Komplex Agreement

The Hesston Corporation of Hesston, Kansas, produces farm equipment and is involved in the sale or licensing of this equipment in several Eastern European countries.[14] Hesston has three domestic divisions and one division located in Coex, France, each of which has its own engineering, manufacturing, and marketing organizations. While most of the sales to the Eastern European countries are sourced from the Coex division, some of the equipment and all of the transfer of technology come from the Hesston division, which is the designer, manufacturer, and marketer of the farm equipment sold by the Hesston Corporation in North America. The division in Coex has a general manager for Eastern European operations, a purchasing director whose sole responsibility is counterpurchases for all of Hesston's divisions, and a person in charge of operations who is responsible for all transfer of technology. The company regards the market for its products to be excellent because of the presence of large state and collective farms. It sells these farms large-capacity hay and forage harvester machines. Its potential for doing business in Eastern Europe is in direct proportion to the potential it has for making counterpurchases in the countries with which it does business.

Hesston agreements in Eastern Europe and the commercial transactions resulting from such agreements can be classified into five categories:

1. Sales agreements with counterpurchases being accomplished by other independent companies (Bulgaria);
2. Sales agreements without counterpurchases, which are extremely limited in nature (Yugoslavia);
3. Sales agreements where counterpurchases are effected by Hesston (Hungary and Yugoslavia);
4. Sales and technology transfer combination agreements where counterpurchases are made by affiliated companies of Hesston (Romania-Fiat); and
5. Sales and technology transfer combination agreements where counterpurchases are made by Hesston (Yugoslavia and Hungary).

The last type of agreement is specifically relevant to Hungary, a country regarded by Hesston as having an excellent market for the company's self-propelled forage harvester machines and, to a more limited degree, the StakHand systems. Both products are rather large-ticket items—one in the $50,000 range; the other in the $30,000 to $40,000 range. Hesston's agreement was entered into with the Komplex Trading Company, a foreign trade organization that acts in behalf of Mezogeptroszt, a large Hungarian farm equipment manufacturing combine. The Hesston agreement calls for the sale of its forage harvester machines to Hungary, with an obligation to counterpurchase agricultural equipment and component parts from Hungary on a 50 percent of sales value basis. Both are licensed by Hesston for production by Mezogeptroszt and are purchased for sale in the Western European and North American markets. These parts and equipment are designed in Hungary in conformance with Hesston's specifications. Hesston considers its agreement with Hungary to be good, not only from the point of view of profitability but from a balance it gains with Western European sales.

Steiger Tractor-RABA Agreement

The Steiger Tractor Company of Fargo, North Dakota, entered into an industrial-cooperation agreement with the Hungarian Railway Carriage and Machine Works (RABA), which has been in business since 1902.[15] RABA manufactures a wide variety of transportation equipment, which is sold all over the world. It manufactures front and rear axles of various designs that can be installed in trucks, tractors, construction vehicles, and various kinds of agricultural tractors. It also manufactures heavy-duty trucks, agricultural tractors, and railroad carriages and such agricultural implements as plows, disk harrows, and planters. The planters, which are air powered, consist of two eight-row planter units linked together by a special pull frame. In one aggregate the units can plant soybeans, corn, or sunflowers and simultaneously apply fertilizers, herbicides, and insecticides. RABA produces several types of diesel engines that are exported to Western Europe and has entered into an industrial-cooperation agreement with the West German iron and steel industrial conglomerate Mannesmann to produce diesel engines for use in road vehicles such as dump trucks.

Steiger and RABA entered into a cooperation agreement to produce tractors. Under the terms of the agreement, RABA has the exclusive right to sell in Hungary Steiger-type agricultural tractors manufactured by RABA, using Steiger CKD units. The tractors are called RABA-Steiger tractors. Under the agreement RABA also has the nonexclusive right to sell RABA-Steiger tractors in the other

Eastern European countries. Further, RABA has the right to export from Hungary on a nonexclusive basis the RABA-Steiger Cougar 11 tractor and may sell these throughout the world, with the exception of the Western hemisphere. However, RABA is free to sell the RABA-Steiger Cougar 11 tractor in the United States. RABA has agreed to sell agricultural tractor axles to Steiger, and Steiger has agreed to sell the CKD units of Steiger agricultural tractors to RABA. Steiger also agreed to deliver drawings and other documents as well as to render technical assistance to RABA in connection with the manufacture by RABA and sale to Steiger of transfer cases used in the Steiger-type tractor. RABA, by the same token, agreed to furnish Steiger drawings for different types of axles as well as to render technical assistance to Steiger for the manufacture of the axles.

Other Cooperation Agreements

Coca-Cola has a licensing agreement with state-owned enterprises in Hungary for the bottling of Coca-Cola.[16] These agreements are similar to the ones that the company has concluded with bottling companies all over the world. The contract grants the bottling company the right to produce and sell Coca-Cola within a certain specified territory. Hungarian bottling companies purchase the Coca-Cola concentrate from one of its concentrate plants, which are located throughout Western Europe. Its concentrate price is set at a level sufficient to cover its production cost, the cost of its services to the Hungarian bottling companies, a portion of its overhead at the Western European concentrate plant, and a profit element. The bottling companies pay for this concentrate in hard currency and are charged an original license fee. Coca-Cola is willing to help Hungary and the other Eastern European countries with which it has licensing agreements generate foreign exchange through counterpurchase arrangements in which it purchases locally produced goods that it resells in Western Europe or the United States. For example, at present Coca-Cola is selling large quantities of Polish beer both in Western Europe and the United States. Although countertrade is expensive, without it Coca-Cola feels that its business with Eastern Europe would be restricted.

Levi Strauss, manufacturer of one of the world's most ubiquitous products, blue jeans, has entered into an industrial-cooperation agreement with five Hungarian partners that involves the production of its quality jeans in a factory located in the town of Marcali, Hungary.[17] Approximately 40 percent of the units produced are sold in the Hungarian market, and the remaining 60 percent are sold outside Hungary. The purpose of entering into a contract with Hungarian manufacturers was threefold: to place the company's products in the Hungarian market, to secure a reasonably inexpensive source of production, and to penetrate the markets of other Eastern European countries. Levi Strauss receives a royalty payment for each garment produced and sold in Hungary or elsewhere, and, in addition, it receives garments for resale at attractive prices. With considerable justification the company feels that the potential for doing business in Eastern Europe is enormous. Everyone is a potential customer for jeans, a symbol of the proletarian classes. Strauss has no objection to countertrade and feels that it is the primary vehicle through which to enter the Eastern European markets.

Coca-Cola is not the only soft drink manufacturer operating in Hungary. Both Canada Dry and Pepsi-Cola have concluded licensing agreements with the Hungarian foreign-trade organization Hungarofruct to supply soft drink concentrates and technical know-how. Canada Dry is responsible for the maintenance of quality control standards and for the development of advertising and publicity of ginger ale within Hungary. Payment involves a 100 percent countertrade agreement, with Canada Dry accepting Hungarian-made fruit juice concentrates, which will be marketed in the United States and Canada. Canada Dry is also to furnish technology for Hungarian fruit drinks, which it and Hungarofruct will jointly market in both Eastern and Western Europe.[18]

Pepsi-Cola has licensing agreements not only with Hungary but also with Poland and other Eastern European countries. In the Soviet Union Pepsi-Cola installed a high-speed bottling plant that produced 50 million bottles of Pepsi in 1976. Additional plants were installed, and in January 1978 Pepsi-Cola signed an agreement with the Russians to double the number of bottling plants to ten by 1980. Total output by 1980 should be around 30 million cases. Pepsi-Cola also agreed to counterpurchase from 200,000 to 1 million cases of vodka, which would bring annual sales of vodka in the United States to around $100 million by 1980. Pepsi-Cola has used its operations in the Soviet Union as a springboard to enter other markets. In Hungary Pepsi-Cola supplies syrup concentrate, machinery, and technology, including quality control. It is also responsible for advertising and publicity. Countertrade is involved in the Pepsi-Cola-Hungarian agreement, with Pepsi agreeing to take tomato juice concentrate, which it will market in the United States, and tires and film.[19]

Pepsi-Cola has been one of the U.S. pioneers in East-West industrial cooperation. There are several key elements in Pepsi's successful penetration of Eastern Europe. One such element is perseverance, for it took Pepsi-Cola almost 15 years before an initial agreement was consummated. It took ten years of exhibiting the soft drink at the Leipzig Fair in East Germany, at a cost of over $50,000, before interest was expressed. There was also a willingness to accept countertrade as a means of gaining access to Eastern European markets. The company promotes Eastern European consumer products in Western markets, thus creating a measure of goodwill in the East. There is an insistence on quality control, and Pepsi's franchises in Eastern Europe are the same as in any Western market in maintaining quality. Pepsi provides technical assistance, training, and marketing aids. Samples of the syrup and water are sent to West Germany for testing. There is regular on-site inspection by Pepsi's engineering department. Pepsi-Cola is also skilled at negotiation, an expertise it has gained through continued involvement in Eastern Europe. Pepsi's vice-president for Eastern Europe says that personal relations between negotiators have reached a point where both sides can openly joke about each other's negotiating ploys.

Countertrade

Hungarian countertrade practices are similar to those of the other Eastern European countries, since there is also the need to conserve hard currency. However, Hungary possesses an advantage over the other countries in that Hungarian goods are generally of good quality, span the country's entire production range, and come from above-target production. Hungarian industrial enterprises, such as RABA, have well-developed export programs and produce products of good quality and long-standing tradition that are well known in Western Europe. However, in terms of the value of countertrade transactions with Western firms, Hungary lags behind the other Eastern European countries. Planned imports of technology for which hard currency has been allocated are free from countertrade requirements. As hard-currency indebtedness to the West has increased, Hungary has started to push for increased countertrade arrangements with Western firms. Transactions that do not receive the highest priority under the Hungarian five-year plan may require the full 100 percent acceptance of Hungarian products in countertrade, with emphasis placed on hard-currency compensation.

Countertrade was involved in the industrial-cooperation agreements between Hesston and Komplex and between RABA and Steiger. Hesston agreed to counterpurchase agricultural equipment and component parts from Hungary, and Steiger agreed to purchase agricultural tractor axles. Levi Strauss agreed to purchase jeans, and Coca-Cola purchases and sells Hungarian beer. Most of Hungary's countertrade transactions involve the acquisition of licenses, know-how, and equipment, with payment in a resultant Hungarian product. Vauxhall of Great Britain provided licensing and know-how to the Hungarians for the manufacture of truck axles and, in return, agreed to purchase a set number of axles. The Tokai Metals Company of Japan provided Hungary with a rolling mill for producing aluminum foil and agreed to purchase the aluminum foil. The West German mining, iron, and steel conglomerate Mannesmann entered into a licensing and know-how agreement with RABA to produce bus engines, which Mannesmann will purchase at a rate of 9,000 a year. Sometimes the cooperative arrangement works in reverse. The Hungarian enterprise Komplex entered into an agreement with the Swedish firm Alpha-Laval to deliver a cheese plant in exchange for Swedish dairy equipment.

FUTURE POTENTIAL FOR
INDUSTRIAL COOPERATION

The future potential for industrial cooperation between Western business firms and Hungarian state enterprises and foreign-trade organizations appears good. The export-oriented development of Hungarian heavy industry and a selective policy of industrial transformation of the economy will continue to involve a large demand for imports. Favorable market opportunities exist for Western firms offering advanced technology. Industrial sectors targeted for the highest amount of state investment under the economic plan include the following: chemicals, machine tools, heavy machinery, electric power, and food processing, with emphasis placed on the mechanization of packaging, materials handling, and transport. Industrial-cooperation agreements will be encouraged for projects in all of these areas. An increasingly important role is given to cooperation agreements that are more advanced and complex than simple sales contracts and meet the requirements of Hungarian industry. The heavy-machinery industry, for example, expects to double the number of industrial-co-operation agreements with Western firms in the period 1978-80. They intend to broaden the types of agreements beyond licensing to include joint marketing and joint production for which new outlets can be found, particularly in the economically developing countries.

The potential for continued business relations between East and West is circumscribed to a considerable degree by the rapid increase in the debt of the East to Western governments and commercial banks. A shortage of Western hard currency is endemic to all of the Eastern European countries, including Hungary. The hard-currency debt of Hungary to the West was $3.0 billion by the end of 1977. By 1979 the hard-currency debt had increased to an estimated $4.1 billion.[20] The ratio of debt service to exports for 1977 was 0.44, which is higher than the conventional banker's rule that a ratio in excess of 0.25 be regarded as excessive. The ratio for Hungary is among the highest for the Eastern European countries and is exceeded only by Bulgaria and Poland. The ratio of net debt to exports for Hungary in 1976 was 1.5 to 1.0, which can be compared with an average ratio of 1.6 to 1.0

for all of the Eastern European countries and was exceeded by Bulgaria, East Germany, and Poland.[21] Heavy investment requirements for the modernization of capital stock have been a source of pressure on the Hungarian economy during the 1970s, and this pressure is expected to continue in this decade. Hungary will have to depend on growing exports of manufactures.

However, there are some positive factors to consider. Hungarian-manufactured products are generally of good quality and are well known, particularly in Western Europe. The Hungarians are actively pursuing closer commercial ties with the West and are interested in concluding more industrial-cooperation agreements. Priority is given in planning to industrial cooperation, and incentives are provided to Western firms to engage in cooperation agreements. Hungary also enjoys MFN status with the United States, which provides it with at least some opportunity to expand exports on the scale needed to cope with debt-service requirements. Credit policies of the United States and Western Europe may well have some impact upon industrial cooperation. During the current period of inflation, as available funds for loans become tighter, there will be increased competition among all borrowers, socialist or otherwise. So far, the distribution of credit has been handled mainly by the market—that is, the decisions of Western commercial banks. But as the supply of credit becomes more restricted, as the United States and Western Europe attempt to cope with inflation, priorities will have to be developed concerning who will get credit.

SUMMARY

At least as measured by Hungarian attitudes toward concluding industrial-cooperation agreements, the climate is reasonably propitious for U.S. and Western European business firms. Hungary introduced joint-venture legislation in 1971, thus developing a novel form of industrial cooperation between capitalist and socialist enterprises. However, the hoped-for gains never materialized. The very foundation of the socialist state form of government does not really permit the true joint venture. Although Hungary, Romania, and Poland to a more circumscribed degree have laws permitting joint ventures, they are not joint ventures in the true sense, because the Western partner cannot really own any part of them. It cannot fire employees because they fail to do their jobs; this is done throughout Eastern Europe by workers' committees. Profits from a joint venture are often very problematical because it works in hard currency. At the Eastern European end there is the problem that joint ventures could prove the supremacy of Western economic and management

methods over the state-run and often inflexible methods of the socialist enterprises. There appears to be a somewhat limited role for
joint ventures in the future.

Hungary has been in the vanguard of the Eastern European countries in terms of the number of agreements concluded with Western
firms for nonequity forms of industrial cooperation. Many of these
agreements are licensing and know-how arrangements with provision
for partial repayment of fees in the form of output. In 1975 the Hungarian machine industry alone acquired 145 foreign licenses. The
Hungarian manufacturing sector has concluded the bulk of cooperation
agreements with Western firms and provides the majority of Hungarian
exports to the West. In 1977 industrial-cooperation agreements with
Western firms accounted for 25 percent of the Hungarian machine industry exports to the West. The sectors that have been the most important areas of cooperation are those that continue to receive the
highest priorities under the economic plan—nonelectrical machinery
and equipment, transport equipment, electrical machinery, electronics, and chemicals.

NOTES

1. The interministerial committee is composed of the chairman of the National Planning Office, a representative of the National
Committee for Technological Development, the minister of metallurgy
and machine industry, a deputy minister nominated by the minister of
finance, the president of the Hungarian National Bank, and the secretary of state for foreign trade, who acts as chairman.

2. Ministry of Finance, Decree no. 28.

3. Hungarian Chamber of Commerce, Regulations Concerning
Foreign Commercial Ventures in Hungary (Budapest: Lapkiado Val-
lalat, 1979).

4. Hungarian Chamber of Commerce, Hungarian Exporter 28
(July-August 1978): 9.

5. Business International, Solving East European Business
Problems, (Geneva, Switzerland: Business International, February
1977), p. 98.

6. Data provided by the Corning Company.

7. Information provided by the Dow Chemical Corporation.

8. Financial Times of London, World Business Weekly, vol.
2, February 5-11, 1979.

9. Hungarian Chamber of Commerce, Hungarian Exporter 28
(September-October 1978): 9.

10. International Development Research Center, "Technology
Transfer: Statistical Findings and Analysis" (chap. 4) (Study prepared
for the Bureau of East-West Trade, U.S. Department of Commerce,
Indiana University, October 1975), tables 1-3.

11. Ibid., table 2.

12. Philip Morris, Annual Stockholders' Report, 1978, pp. 5-6.

13. Data provided by Philip Morris.

14. Data provided by the Hesston Corporation.

15. Data provided by the Steiger Tractor Company.

16. Data provided by Coca-Cola.

17. Data provided by Levi Strauss.

18. Hungarian Chamber of Commerce, Hungarian Exporter 28 (November-December 1978): 10.

19. Data provided by the Pepsi-Cola Corporation.

20. U.S., Congress, Joint Economic Committee, Issues in East-West Commercial Relations, 95th Cong., 2d sess., 1979, p. 24.

21. Brookings Institution, Economic Relations between East and West: Prospects and Problems (Washington, D.C.: Brookings Institution, 1978), p. 23.

6
INDUSTRIAL COOPERATION
IN ROMANIA

Romania, unlike the other Council for Mutual Economic Assistance (CMEA) countries, has attempted to maintain a certain degree of independence from Soviet economic and political dominance. Although Moscow can and will set general parameters beyond which no political leadership within the Soviet sphere of influence can safely venture, Romanian President Nicolae Ceauşescu has pushed Romania toward relations with many countries, including some that are in Moscow's disfavor. Romania has maintained close economic and political ties to the People's Republic of China, one country that is at continuous loggerheads with the Soviet Union, even though both are of the same political persuasion. It was the first socialist country to open diplomatic relations with West Germany and enjoys close economic ties with other capitalist countries. Romanian-U.S. relations have been quite good, with trade between the two countries reaching a record level in 1978. Continued relations with Israel at a time when all the other countries in Eastern Europe have broken diplomatic relations with the "Zionist imperialist state," coupled with support of China, have made Romania suspect in Moscow's eyes and have resulted in increased Soviet pressure for more political conformity—pressure that is resisted by Ceauşescu.

Romania has had to transform itself from an agrarian to an industrial society. Before World War II there were small centers of industrialization in what was one of Europe's greatest masses of rural poverty. Romania suffered much from its participation on the side of the Germans during the war, including the loss of some of its more prosperous regions to the Soviet Union. After the war there was a period of recovery, followed by the establishment of a Communist party and the development of a Stalinist economic program of rapid industrial development. Incorporation into the Eastern economic bloc was forced. Production goals were based primarily on the construction and development of domestic basic industries and expansion of the production of capital goods, to the detriment of producing goods for consumer use. The substance of the first two five-year plans was in accordance with these goals: a predominant encouragement of capital goods accompanied by a clear neglect of private consumption. In the light of existing foreign-exchange deficits, agriculture was expected to produce more of the high-quality products necessary for domestic consumption.

During the period 1950-70, the Romanian economy made substantial economic gains. Total industrial production increased by 1,000 percent, and agricultural production increased by 225 percent. However, most of the gain in industrial production occurred in heavy industry, while the consumer goods industry showed a much more moderate rate of growth. After many years of relative deprivation, the Romanian people developed a desire for higher material consumption and better services. A higher living standard was considered more important than limited political participation. Although Romania had made rapid industrial gains, particularly in comparison with the prewar period, per capita income and living standards were generally lower than those of the other Eastern European countries, with the exception of Bulgaria. Thus, Ceauşescu has had to press forward with a drive for modernization since much of his popularity rests on the idea of steady progress and development. He seeks to lay the material bases of socialism through rapid economic development. To facilitate the process of modernization, Romania has had to import the technology necessary to improve social and economic conditions. A trend toward greater industrial cooperation with the West has developed, beginning around the latter part of the 1960s.

Joint-equity ventures and industrial-cooperation agreements represent to the Romanians a vehicle for the attainment of a number of goals. First, they are used to import badly needed Western technology. Second, they represent a way in which to produce and export products to Western markets. Third, they provide a means to break through various political, economic, and organizational constraints that impinge upon Romanian trade with the West. Fourth, the joint-venture and industrial-cooperation agreements may be used as partial substitutes for conventional foreign trade as well as direct capital transfers in countries whose currencies are inconvertible and where existing production patterns place a constraint on the volume of goods that can be produced for export. Finally, these arrangements enable Romania or any socialist country to have the advantage of benefiting from the implicit calculations by a Western partner as to what is worth producing and what can be exported for hard currency to compensate for deficits in the Romanian balance of payments.

JOINT VENTURES IN ROMANIA

Romania passed a law called Law no. 1 permitting joint-equity ventures in 1971,[1] thus becoming the first CMEA country to allow foreign private investment. There were several reasons for passing the joint-venture law. First, industrial development in Romania had generally lagged behind the levels achieved in the other CMEA countries. Second, there was, and is, a paucity of natural resources, which necessitated imports of raw materials, equipment, and technology. This contributed to increased deficits in the country's balance of trade. Despite efforts to promote foreign trade, Romania was unable to increase its share of the Western market. Therefore, the Romanians deemed it necessary to institute a new legal framework to increase the potential for trade with the West. The banking system was revised to create the Bank of Foreign Trade, which assumed responsibility for international banking functions formerly held by the National Bank of Romania. Foreign-trade organizations were reorganized, and the Ministry of Foreign Trade was given more latitude in decision making. Romanian industries were reorganized along lines similar to those adopted by other Eastern European countries in that they were formed into industrial combines. Rules were liberalized concerning the holding and use of convertible currency.

Law no. 1 was supplemented by various decrees that helped to define the status of joint-venture agreements. Decree no. 424 of 1972 deals with the organization and operation of joint ventures in Romania. It allows for the creation of joint-equity ventures in the fields of industry, agriculture, construction, tourism, and transport. It also defines the objectives that are to be achieved in order for a joint venture to be permitted. The venture would result in the creation of products that fulfill home-market needs and thus reduce or eliminate the need for imports with their concomitant drain on hard currency. Then there are projects that result in the creation of goods for export, which would improve the potential to earn hard currency. Projects that also require large amounts of fixed capital receive high priority with respect to joint ventures. Ventures that improve the state of Romanian technology or promote and develop scientific research activities are also given preference. Joint-venture agreements usually satisfy some need on the part of Romania, such as the production of industrial chains, which had to be imported. The joint venture Romelite, formed with the West German firm Franz Kohmaier, was created to produce chains for industrial use in Romania.

Decree no. 424 also outlines the nature and extent of Romanian and foreign participation in joint ventures. The Romanian share in the registered capital has to be at least 51 percent. A joint venture can be either a joint stock company or a limited liability company;

there is no preference as to the type that the partners may choose. Romanian participation in a joint venture can include combines, trusts, groups of enterprises and factories, and foreign-trade organizations responsible under Romanian law for foreign-trade activities. The Romanian government guarantees the repatriation of profits of the foreign partner and authorizes their transfer through the Romanian Foreign Trade Bank. Also guaranteed is the value of shares in the venture that are transferred to foreign accounts. Both profit and share repatriation are subject to prior state claims such as taxes and contributions to social insurance. Finally, joint ventures are supposed to provide annual and five-year plans of economic and financial goals. These plans are coordinated with the annual and five-year plans of the Romanian state.

Decree no. 424 has other provisions as well. The contribution of the foreign partner may be in the form of financial capital, a share in goods, or industrial property or other rights. The Romanian contribution may include the equivalent value of the right to use of land that the government makes available to the joint company. Expenses are to be paid in the currency agreed upon in the contract. Raw materials and supplies can be purchased internally in the agreed-upon currency or imported. Output can be sold in the agreed-upon currency in the domestic market and either directly or through foreign-trade organizations in foreign markets. All foreign currency payments must be made from the company's own reserve currency or from loans. A reserve fund must be created from a portion of the profits. Remaining profits after deduction of the reserve fund and taxes are to be distributed in proportion to the shares of invested capital, with a portion set aside for the future expansion of the company. The decree also contains provisions concerning the rights of workers consistent with Romanian law and provides procedures for litigation and for dissolution and liquidation of the joint company.

Decree no. 425 deals with taxation of profits of joint ventures. All joint projects are taxed at a rate of 30 percent. Taxes are based on income less expenses, with an allowance made for a tax-free reserve fund deduction, which is to be accumulated at the rate of 5 percent a year up to 25 percent of invested capital. When profits are reinvested for at least five years in the joint venture, a 20 percent reinvestment deduction is applied to the 30 percent rate, so that profits are actually taxed at a rate of 24 percent. When profits are repatriated by a foreign partner back to the home country, an additional tax of 10 percent is added. However, to facilitate the operations of the joint venture, Romania allows an exemption of customs duties on all joint-venture-related imports. A full exemption from the basic profit tax can be granted under certain conditions. For example, a full exemption may be given on an individual basis for the first year in which profits are accumulated, and reduction of the tax by one-half can be made for the two following calendar years.

Other provisions of Romanian joint-venture legislation deal with such areas as personnel practices, the obligations of management, defaults and damages, and dissolution and liquidation. Personnel practices are of prime importance, because it is necessary to project the number of employees consistent with the state economic plan. Joint ventures depend upon local authorities for the supply of labor. Skilled workers have to be taken away from other Romanian enterprises, which usually do not release their best people. The establishment of appropriate wage rates has to be set forth in considerable detail and has to be approved by the Romanian government. By the same token, salaries of Western and Romanian managerial personnel have to be established in the legal agreement. This can create a problem, for there is a considerable difference in what Western and Romanian managers receive in income. Then employee functional areas have to be designated. Friction can occur when responsibilities are not clearly delineated. The handling of labor grievances is also defined in the Romanian laws; however, grievances are minimal, since Romanian law permits no strikes, and workers are required to work three shifts.

The obligations of management also have to be spelled out in the agreement. For example, the agreement between Control Data Corporation and the Romanian government states that the latter is to provide the managing director for a period of three years, subject to renewal upon the approval of both parties. The assistant director is appointed by Control Data, subject to renewal after two years if both parties approve. There are also a board of directors and a managing committee, with the latter selected by the former. The managing committee is responsible for overseeing the general management of the joint venture. The chairman of the board of directors alternates between a Western and Romanian representative, but there is no control given over the management of the venture. Finally, there is what is called an assembly of shareholders, which consists of the Romanian government and the Western company. The extent of participation in the assembly is based upon the extent of the contributions of each party to the joint agreement, or, in the case of Control Data, 55 percent for Romania and 45 percent for the company. The assembly is supposed to be called within three months after the close of the venture's financial year and concerns itself with the distribution of profits.

Defaults and damages are also covered in the joint-venture laws. There are provisions that govern damages against third parties or given by third parties and provisions that govern the failure of one party to the joint-venture agreement to fulfill its obligations. Provision is also made that the parties should attempt to eliminate problems arising out of default through mutual consultation. Romanian law provides for the creation of an arbitration committee to adjudicate disputes. This committee is appointed by the Ministry of Commerce and Industry. Decisions may be appealed before the Romanian law courts. Arbitration awards are binding, but a limit is placed on the amount of damages payable by either party. Both parties must bear the general expenses of arbitration, which take the form of an arbitration fee. This fee amounts to 1 percent of the amount in dispute, a charge that is low by Western standards. Romania adheres to the 1958 New York convention on the enforcement of arbitration awards. Romanian courts are considered to be unbiased when it comes to the enforcement of arbitration awards, and no cases are known in which a court has had to force a defendant to pay a final award.

Dissolution and liquidation procedures are also spelled out under the Romanian joint-venture laws. There are conditions under which ventures can be dissolved and liquidated. Provision is made for residual obligations of one party to the other in the event of dissolution as well as for residual rights with respect to further manufacturing, marketing, licensing, and patents. All cash contributions, as well as contributed goods, arc valued in the currency agreed upon in the contract of association and statutes. The value of assets other than cash is determined by using foreign-trade prices based on price levels in convertible currency of typical foreign markets. The same criteria are used in the event of dissolution and liquidation, with each party entitled to the pro rata share of its contribution. The Romanian government guarantees the transfer abroad of both venture profits and contributed capital. Land can be contributed by the Romanian partner in the joint venture; in the event of dissolution the land reverts to state ownership. If land is not used as a specific contribution, the venture then has to pay rent to the state for its use.

The dominant feature of a joint venture is the property relationship flowing from equity ownership. Ownership provides security for invested capital and creates a basis for the rights of management. Changes in the economic and political climate, or in the relationship to the Romanian partner, cannot affect the Western partner's right to a share in the profits, or even the assets of the venture. Expropriation is always a possibility, but it is more likely that the state would simply revoke the Western partner's right to do business, forcing a sale at a loss. Should this happen, the Western firm would find that the integration of industry in Romania is so thorough that the only interested buyer would be the Romanian partner, even if there were no collusion among the economic ministries. Thus, joint ventures should have, as a prerequisite, an investment contract into which the Western partner can write as many escape clauses as possible.

Types of Joint Ventures

Overview

As of the end of 1978, there were seven joint ventures between Western firms and Romanian foreign-trade organizations and state enterprises.[2] Control Data Corporation of the United States is a partner in the joint venture Romcontroldata, which produces peripheral elements for computers. Japan's Dai-Nippon established the joint venture Roniprot with the Romanian Industrial Central for Pharmaceutical Dyes and Paints. The purpose of the venture is to produce protein-rich yeast from crude oils as a basis for livestock feed. Renk-Zahnraederfabrik of West Germany entered into a joint venture with the Romanian ICMR Machine Work to produce industrial gears. The Austrian firm Franz Kohmaier is involved in a joint venture to produce chains for industrial use, and Romalfa, an Italian firm, produces industrial fibers along with its Romanian partner in the joint venture Roniprot. Other Western companies participating in joint ventures in Romania are Citroën of France and General Maritime of Libya. A joint venture that failed involved the French company L'Electronique Appliqueé and the Romanian Industrial Central for Electronics and Data Processing Technology. The joint venture Elarom was to manufacture electronic heart pacemakers and monitoring equipment for use in Romania and other socialist countries. Apparently, the Romanians had problems meeting the high quality standards necessary for the heart device.

Romcontroldata Joint Venture

In 1973 the U.S. firm Control Data Corporation of Minneapolis, Minnesota, concluded an agreement to form a joint venture with Romania's Industrial Group for Electronic and Calculating Techniques. The initial contact with Romania was made by Control Data in 1968, when it began to sell its products in the Romanian market. The Romanians at that time were interested in developing their own computer industry and had approached British and French firms, seeking technical assistance and licensing agreements. Control Data expressed an interest in providing the Romanians with technical aid but was deterred by the policies of the U.S. government toward Eastern Europe. Although export controls of U.S. products to Eastern Europe had been relaxed by the Export Administration Act of 1969, computer and computer-related products remained on the controlled list, because they were deemed important to the national interest. Improvement of U.S. economic and political relations in the early 1970s led to some relaxation of control on the part of the U.S. government. Thus, negotiations between Control Data and the Romanians were continued, with turnkey projects and licensing agreements discussed. Eventually the joint-venture form of arrangement was chosen, for Romania had passed its joint-venture law. It was also necessary to receive U.S. government approval for the transfer of technology involved in the production of computers. This approval was secured.

Under the joint-venture agreement, the fully subscribed capital amounted to $4 million, with the Romanians providing $2.2 million and Control Data the remainder—a 55 percent to 45 percent relationship.[3] In addition to the capital subscription, both partners made other contributions, including the provision of cash, land, equipment, servicing, and licensing. These contributions were also delineated as to source, with Control Data supplying equipment, technology, and managerial skills—for a total of 45 percent—and Romania supplying the plant and most of the labor. A computer-manufacturing plant was constructed in Bucharest, and as of 1979, it employs 200 workers. It manufactures a variety of computer peripherals, including a drum-type printer that is one of the factory's main products. These peripherals are sold in Western Europe, the United States, and Eastern Europe. Control Data shares in the proceeds of this joint venture by virtue of being a true-equity partner. No countertrade is involved, but Control Data does purchase a sufficient amount of the factory's output to allow the Romanians to roughly balance the hard currency outflow that results from their purchase of parts and equipment from Control Data.

The problem of pricing in a socialist economy is of a different order of magnitude from that under capitalism. For one thing prices do not determine the allocation of resources to the same extent as in a market economy. The price structure of most products typically consists of production cost, profit of the producer, taxes, and wholesale and retail price markups. Romanian domestic prices within each industry are published by the state in a catalog. Prices are set to cover the average cost of goods—that is, materials, utilities, wages and social taxes, and depreciation, plus an approved profit markup. This markup is set within ranges established by the state and represents what can be considered an industry average. However, higher profit markups are approved for capital-intensive industries such as electronics to provide internal financing, capital repairs, and expansion. But the fact remains that no fully workable price system has been devised in Romania or in any other socialist country. Prices do not reflect factor costs, as rent and interest are not necessarily accounted for in them. Moreover, the use of a single profit rate in the price set for a particular product does not result in a uniform rate of profit for all enterprises, because production costs vary widely.

The joint venture developed certain problems reflecting differences in ideologies between a Western corporation and a state enterprise. One problem involved the setting of a mutually acceptable wage rate. Incentive wages based on productivity standards were opposed by the Romanians on the grounds that superior workers would be lured away from other state-owned enterprises. There was opposition to creating a capitalist enclave where workers would earn much more than other Romanians, thus creating animosity and envy. This was circumvented by playing down wage differentials and playing up working conditions and the novelty of working for a joint U.S.-Romanian enterprise. There was also the problem of who should manage the plant. At the inception of the joint venture, the Romanian manager was given a U.S. assistant, which caused a considerable amount of friction.[4] Eventually the Romanian manager was given supervision of the factory, answering only to a management committee, which meets quarterly. The U.S. presence was gradually lessened. For the first two years of plant operation, there were five U.S. citizens involved in the management process, but none had more than rudimentary skills with the Romanian language. Their number was eventually reduced to two, a director of quality control and a manager of materials, both of whom were on floating loan from Control Data.

There were other problems associated with the creation and operation of the joint venture. For one thing there were restrictions placed by the U.S. government. Export licenses had to be granted by the United States for production of more advanced equipment. U.S. officials were reluctant to permit the sale of technology that might be converted to military use. Up-to-date computer equipment falls into that category. But it is modern computer technology that the Eastern European countries tend to be most interested in, for they want to bolster their economic strength. They also want to sell products that will earn them hard currency for buying more technology and paying off foreign debts. The joint venture suffered an initial setback when its line of card punchers and card readers turned out to be obsolete even before production actually began. After that it was not until early 1975 that Romcontroldata came up with another item, a drum-type printer. It, too, had little appeal to Western buyers with access to more advanced models. Sales were limited to primarily within Romania and other Soviet bloc countries. A dilemma confronted the U.S. and Romanian participants. What the venture could build was obsolete by Western standards and would not sell; what would sell, the U.S. government would not permit it to sell.

Problems of consummating and implementing the joint venture were not limited to U.S. government restrictions. On the Romanian side there were layers of cumbersome bureaucracy with which Control Data had to deal, plus limited access to end-users, insistence upon overly generous credit terms, the inconvertibility of Romanian currency, and social and cultural differences. The bargaining process was laborious, and patience became a necessity for success. On several occasions negotiations between Control Data and the Romanians were on the verge of collapse. As is true in the other socialist countries, Romanian negotiators, with good reason, did not want to assume responsibility for making decisions. Thus, negotiations had to be passed up the line to higher authorities for ultimate approval. Needless to say, this can be a very time-consuming process. The initiative in negotiations devolved to Control Data by default. The securing of supplies also presented some difficulties after the joint venture was started. In purchasing raw materials or semifinished products, it was necessary to wait for the Romanian bureaucracy to decide what prices suppliers could charge. Joint ventures have to pay for raw materials and semifinished products in hard currency, and Romanian authorities have to find the world prices before converting prices from the Romanian currency unit into hard currency.

So far Control Data is the only U.S. firm participating in a Romanian joint venture. The question legitimately arises of whether the joint venture has been successful from Control Data's viewpoint. The answer is that on balance the joint venture is regarded as a success.[5] Although profits were not made during the first years of operation, there were extenuating circumstances, the most important of which was a recession in the West. However, Control Data made a profit in 1978 and expected to repeat its performance in 1979. In addition, there are other factors that Control Data regards as important reasons for its presence in Romania. One such factor is easier penetration of the Eastern European markets. The company enjoys a competitive advantage over other Western firms because of its geographic propinquity to the Eastern markets, and it has branch offices in Moscow and Warsaw. Control Data has achieved a good public-relations image in the other Eastern European countries because of its operations in Romania. Its factory is tangible proof of its presence, and many officials from Eastern Europe have visited the premises. More business has accrued to Control Data as a result of the factory in Romania.

Another factor that Control Data regards as favorable to its operations in Romania is potential access to the China market. Romania, alone among the Eastern European countries, has maintained good political relations with the People's Republic of China. Officials from the People's Republic of China have visited the Control Data plant in Bucharest. Romania also enjoys excellent commercial relations with the Third World countries, a fact that is not lost on Control Data. Romanian state enterprises have been involved in the construction of plants and facilities in Africa and India, affording Control Data potential access to these areas. Finally, there is the Romanian market itself. To some extent it is a captive market, at least as far as Control Data is concerned. The joint venture is a part of the Romanian production and distribution rubric—an integrated and familiar unit. Romanian state enterprises are more prone to deal with a known entity within the country than with more remote Western firms. However, it is difficult to assess just how much the physical presence of the U.S. company adds to its total volume of business.

Future Potential for Joint Ventures

It is difficult to portend the future potential for joint ventures between Western capitalist firms and Romanian enterprises. As mentioned previously, only seven Western firms have consummated joint ventures with Romania, but there are several proposed ventures in various stages of the negotiation process. There are several factors that work to the success of joint ventures. For one thing, the Romanians are most anxious to broaden their contacts with the West. Romania continues its efforts toward rapid industrialization and maintains an annual industrial growth rate of 10 percent.[6] It has shown a strong desire to promote and develop cooperation between Western firms and Romanian enterprises. Second, the failure of any existing joint venture could cause the Romanians considerable embarrassment. Right or wrong, if one of the joint ventures should fail, the Romanians would be held accountable. One joint venture actually has failed, but it was difficult to assess the blame. The French participant blames the Romanians, claiming they could not produce the sophisticated electronic heart pacemaker, and the Romanians blame the French firm, claiming it did not supply the technicians necessary to teach them how to make the pacemaker. It appears, however, that joint ventures are bound to succeed, for the Romanians could not afford the repercussions among Western firms that might invest in the country.

Experiences of existing joint ventures may create some problems for future ventures. One reason for a Western partner's entering into joint-venture agreements is to tap the markets of other Eastern European countries. There appears to be a reluctance on the part of these countries to buy from Romanian joint ventures, even though they could obtain the product at a lower price than if it were purchased from the West. In part this can be explained by the feeling that if it is necessary to give up hard currency, which is what a Romanian joint venture wants, then it is better to give it to the West directly. The assumption is that the Western product is automatically better than anything made in Romania. Then, too, Romania has the reputation among its neighbors for being a socialist maverick. From the standpoint of the interested Western partner, it is desirable to explore the market potentials of the other Eastern European countries before entering into a joint-venture agreement in which output is to be sold in Eastern Europe.

In several ventures considerable delays were experienced before operations began. In one venture involving the Japanese firm Dai-Nippon a delay of two years was experienced, with an original 1977 target date tentatively reset for 1979.[7] One problem involved an absence of supplies, which occurred because joint ventures are excluded from the annual and five-year plans; thus Romanian supply sources were committed under the plans to other purchasers. Another problem involved motivating Romanian workers to complete the plant on schedule. Since wages in joint-venture projects are not supposed to be higher than those set in the state-owned industries, there was no incentive to work harder. These and other problems illustrate the complexity of joint ventures, for there has to be a melding of two completely different political and economic ideologies. These problems may prove to be transitory in nature, something that will be worked out as more experience is gained with joint ventures. But it is more likely that joint ventures, at least as based on the Romanian experience, will play a limited role as far as future industrial cooperation is concerned.

As was mentioned in the Control Data example, dealing with the Romanian bureaucracy can have an inhibiting effect upon joint ventures. Bureaucracy is slow to act in Romania as well as in the other Eastern European countries. But it might be added that, at least in the case of Control Data, the Washington bureaucracy was equally as dilatory. Bureaucratic slowness discourages joint ventures, for word gets to industries. Small companies are almost precluded from participating in joint ventures, because they cannot afford the delays and expenses involved in negotiations. In order to consummate the joint venture, Control Data has to maintain an executive team in Bucharest for an extended period of time. There was a complete turnover in the Romanian negotiating team. The problem of bureaucratic procrastination is not completely insoluble, but patience and perseverance are requirements. There is much to learn about conducting business in an environment foreign to the ideologies of both the Western and Eastern partners. The joint venture occupies an anomalous position within a centrally planned economy.

INDUSTRIAL-COOPERATION AGREEMENTS

Romanian Pursuit of Western Commercial Ties

Romania has actively pursued commercial ties with the West, and nearly 100 Western corporations have offices in Romania. Industrial-cooperation agreements have been concluded with a number of Western firms. Romania promotes these agreements because it enables them to update their manufacturing and product technology, allows them to add value locally, and reduces their hard-currency requirements. Romanian leaders seek a key to rapid industrial growth, and Western firms are interested in the receptivity shown by Romania toward cooperation. Although bureaucracy in all of the socialist countries creates much red tape and time-consuming delays, apparently in Romania the receptivity factor at least tends to compensate for delay. Romania offers such advantages as contacts with the People's Republic of China and the Third World countries of Africa and Asia. There is also a perceived degree of political stability in Romania, which is of importance to Western firms. In comparison with Poland, where the hold of the Edward Gierek regime on the people is rather tenuous, there is political and economic stability in Romania.

A majority of Romanian industrial-cooperation agreements have been concluded with Western European firms, with West German firms being the most prominent in terms of numbers. The West German firm Maschinenfabrik of Augsburg-Nürnberg concluded an agreement with the Romanian foreign trade organization Industrialimport to license production of diesel engines.[8] A West German consortium has created an Institute for Nuclear Technology in Pitesti, Romania, to develop fuel cycling in thermal reactors. Austrian firms, given their location, have also been active in industrial-cooperation agreements with Romania. The Austrian firm Ludwig Engel and the Romanian state enterprise Romchim entered into a joint production agreement to produce hard-rubber cases. Scandinavian firms, particularly Finnish and Swedish, have concluded several large cooperation agreements with Romania. A Finnish consortium has entered into a cooperation agreement with Romanian state enterprises to construct oil-drilling rigs and mining and ore-dressing equipment.

U.S.-Romanian Industrial-Cooperation Agreements

Although the bulk of Romanian industrial-cooperation agreements have been concluded with Western European firms, there has been considerable U.S. business involvement. A study prepared by the International Research Center of Indiana University for the U.S. Bureau of East-West Trade indicated that as of the winter of 1975 some 102 cooperation agreements had been signed or were in the process of negotiation between U.S. and Romanian enterprises.[9] The most common form of industrial cooperation was the licensing agreement: of the 55 agreements concluded, 25 involved licenses, with direct lump-sum cash payments being the most common form of remuneration.[10]

Royalties and payment in products were other common forms of remuneration. Turnkey agreements were also popular, with more than 20 completed or in the process of completion as of 1975. In most cases U.S. firms were the prime contractors; in two cases, U.S. firms were subcontractors. Coproduction agreements were of limited consequence, with only 2 under contract or concluded by 1975 and 2 in the process of negotiation. Other forms of industrial-cooperation agreements, in particular subcontracting and joint marketing, were unimportant as far as U.S. business was concerned.

As was true for the other Eastern European countries included in the study, large U.S. firms concluded the bulk of the cooperation agreements with Romania. Of the 102 agreements signed or in the process of negotiation as of 1975, 71 involved companies among For-tune's 500 select list of largest firms. [11] Most, if not all, of these firms would qualify as multinationals. Experiences on the part of Control Data and the Clark Equipment Company (cited below) tend to confirm the notion that the large companies have the resources and staying power necessary to carry cooperation agreements to a successful conclusion. The costs of market entry are high because negotiations require an excessive amount of top-executive time, and risks are high because of market uncertainties. Medium-sized and smaller firms come in after the door has been opened by the large firms. Smaller, specialty firms may be brought in by large firms as independent subcontractors after the initial agreement has been signed. Many of the medium-sized and smaller firms also qualify as multinationals. In fact more than 80 percent of the U.S. firms included in the Indiana study qualified as multinationals and derived on the average 34 percent of annual sales from foreign operations.

Clark Equipment Company-Universal Tractor

The Clark Equipment Company of Buchanan, Michigan, is a manufacturer of material-handling equipment, construction equipment, and, to a lesser extent, agricultural equipment. In a separate industrial group Clark manufactures axles and transmissions for construction equipment for sale in domestic and foreign markets. It operates a manufacturing subsidiary in Bruges, Belgium, which manufactures one model line of construction equipment transmissions. However, the company felt that it was at a competitive disadvantage as it has neither subsidiaries nor licensees manufacturing its broad line of transmissions in Europe. In order to better penetrate the Western European market and simultaneously participate in the Eastern European market for transmissions of Clark design, Clark started negotiations with the Romanian foreign-trade organization Universal Tractor in 1973. [12] After two years of negotiations, which were at times frustrating, Clark signed a series of industrial-cooperation agreements with Universal Tractor. These agreements were as follows:

1. A licensing agreement to provide for the manufacture—in a plant to be built at Brasov, Romania—of large transmission models not built in Bruges and for the joint design of two transmission models of the type Clark did not produce,

2. A trademark agreement permitting the transmissions made under the license agreement to carry Clark trademarks subject to quality control assurance that would be administered by Clark, and

3. A marketing agreement whereby Clark would purchase transmissions from the Romanian plant for its European subsidiary manufacturing construction equipment and for resale to Western European customers of Clark. [13]

The Romanians have now completed the transmission plant at a cost of about $100 million and have started production. Clark's relationship with the Romanians has been excellent. The jointly designed transmission met and exceeded all expectations and is now in production, with the quality of workmanship rated as very good. The sale of Clark components for transmissions that the Romanians are starting to produce and for transmissions not being produced in Romania has been several million dollars a year. This has meant, in addition to Clark's license fees, a considerable contribution to the U.S.-Romanian balance of trade. Clark estimates the sales of its U.S.-made components to the Romanian licensee will continue at several million dollars per year in the forseeable future. Additionally, it has received a considerable number of orders for machine tools and heat-treat furnaces in connection with a similar license arrangement for manufacture of Clark-design axles in another Eastern European country; it anticipates that the Romanian agreement may provide considerable sales opportunities in these product areas. Clark states that its license agreement with Romania has met and exceeded all of its expectations. It has built a plant in Rockingham, North Carolina, to expand its domestic production capacity to meet growing U.S. demand and to furnish component parts to its Romanian licensee.

The main problem, as Clark views continued industrial cooperation with the Eastern European countries, is the hard-currency indebtedness common to all of them, which has hampered sales from the United States. However, since Romania received most-favored-nation (MFN) treatment, its exports to the United States, which are mostly in the form of raw materials, have increased to such an extent that they are approaching a U.S.-Romanian balance of payments. The future for U.S.-Romanian industrial cooperation, at least from the standpoint of the Clark Equipment Company, appears to be quite good.

Other Agreements

A number of U.S. firms have concluded various forms of industrial-cooperation agreements with Romania. USS Engineers and Consultants (UEC), an affiliate of US Steel, has scientific and technical cooperation agreements with both Poland and Romania. In both countries UEC provides technical assistance and know-how for the layout, design, procurement, erection, start-up, and operation of silicon-steel-producing facilities.[14] The contracts with Poland and Romania are for a period of three years, and no countertrade is involved. The Norton Company, manufacturer of grinding wheels and coated abrasives, has cooperation agreements with Poland, Romania, and the Soviet Union. In the Soviet Union the agreements cover technological know-how and machinery and equipment to produce the most advanced pulpstones available in the Eastern bloc countries.[15] In Romania Norton provides engineering assistance to produce equipment necessary to manufacture coated abrasives. It is also responsible for the development of a plant to produce the abrasives, which are used for metalworking operations in basic steel-rolling processes, as well as plant start-up and tests to prove plant capability to make a specified quality and volume of product that the company guarantees. There is no countertrade involved in the cooperation agreement.

General Tire has two industrial-cooperation agreements with Romania. One agreement is for the supply of design, engineering, equipment, and technical assistance to establish a radial construction passenger and truck tire-tube factory unit.[16] The second agreement calls for the supply of radial passenger and truck manufacturing technology and all updating of the same for a period of ten years on a fixed-annual-fee basis. The agreements are for the supply of a plant and for supply of technical know-how for fixed fees, with some countertrade involved. Countertrade is handled by a specialized third party. General Tire is not averse to countertrade, taking the position that trade should be developed on the basis of a two-way flow. Energy-source materials and vital raw materials should be made a part of in-flow trade. This would avoid negative trade balances of the Eastern European countries vis-à-vis the United States and increase their borrowing power and purchasing capacity. Many, if not the majority, of the U.S. corporations operating in Eastern Europe do not share this view of countertrade.

Through its Island Creek Coal Company, Occidental Petroleum has entered into a 20-year industrial-cooperation agreement with Romania to construct a metallurgical-grade coal mine.[17] Island Creek received from the Romanian government the basic capital to construct the coal mine. The Romanians were willing to use scarce capital resources to secure a long-term supply of a very scarce commodity. Special situations where the critical need for a commodity overrides capital scarcity are not very frequent. Romania has agreed to purchase one-third of the production of the coal mine over the 20-year period. It will make predelivery payments for the coal up to $53 million. If capital required to complete the mine exceeds $53 million, Romania will make further predelivery payments equivalent to one-third of capital expenditures in excess of $53 million. Romania will make further payments for coal equal to the cost of production at the time such coal is shipped and has an option to purchase an additional one-third of the mine's production at fair-market value. Island Creek will receive normal profits on two-thirds of the production of the mine and will receive a lesser profit on the one-third of production involved in the advance-payment mechanism. No countertrade is involved in the agreement.

The Romanians place much emphasis on countertrade arrangements as a part of industrial cooperation. Attitudes of U.S. firms toward countertrade vary. Gulf General Atomic, a subsidiary of Gulf Oil, sold a research reactor to Romania and installed all of the necessary facilities. It entered into a countertrade agreement with Romania to purchase a certain amount of Romanian goods over a stipulated period of time.[18] If it was unable to purchase the goods as stipulated in the contract, a penalty was assessed on the purchase price of the reactor, which reduced its price. However, Gulf Oil took the position that acceptance of countertrade was a means of entering a developed market in which there were few U.S. participants. A similar view is expressed by the Coca-Cola Company.[19] It regards countertrade as an expensive way to do business, but without it the potential for doing business in Eastern Europe is restricted. Coca-Cola regards the potential for its products in Eastern Europe to be enormous, but it will only be able to tap this potential if and when it is able to find a solution to the difficult problem of generating sufficient amounts of foreign exchange through countertrade or similar transactions.

THE FUTURE POTENTIAL FOR
U.S.-ROMANIAN INDUSTRIAL COOPERATION

Of all the Eastern European countries, Romania may offer the most potential for various forms of industrial cooperation for U.S. business firms. U.S.-Romanian political relations have been generally quite good, beginning with the visit of President Richard Nixon to Romania in 1969. The tempo of U.S.-Romanian economic relations quickened in 1973 with the visit of President Ceausescu to the United States. During his visit a joint statement on economic, industrial, and technical cooperation was signed, containing a provision for the creation of the bilateral U.S.-Romanian Economic Commission. The Trade Act of 1974 granted Romania MFN status and cleared the way for Romanian access to Export-Import Bank credits. Section 402 of the Trade Act, which prohibits the special granting of favored economic treatment to any Communist country that does not permit its citizens the right to emigrate, has been waived in the case of Romania. The U.S.-Romanian Trade Agreement, also signed in 1974, is an important factor in stimulating commercial relations. It has been extended to 1981, because concessions in trade and services have been maintained during the existence of the agreement. There was a quid pro quo relationship on the part of both the United States and Romania in terms of reductions in tariff barriers.

Romanian interest in an expansion of contacts with U.S. business firms was expedited by President Ceausescu's second visit to the United States in April 1978. There was a reaffirmation of commitments to promote expansion of trade and economic cooperation between the United States and Romania. During his visit to the United States, President Ceausescu made visits to several U.S. cities to discuss potential business opportunities in Romania with various business firms. The desire for U.S. business involvement can be linked to the current Romanian five-year plan, which calls for annual rates of real economic growth in excess of 10 percent based on investment ratios of nearly one-third of national income.[20] In order to come close to accomplishing these high growth rates, there is an increased demand for investment goods and technology from the Western market economies. There is the need to earn foreign currency to pay for imports of technology. The way in which this can be done is to find export markets for the output of Romanian goods, which can be brought about through increased industrial cooperation with Western firms.

There are other factors that may portend increased industrial cooperation between U.S. and Romanian enterprises. First, U.S. exports to and imports from Romania have shown rather substantial increases, reflecting improving trade opportunities. In 1970 U.S. exports to Romania amounted to $66 million; in 1978 exports amounted to $317 million. On the other side of the coin, U.S. imports from Romania amounted to $13 million in 1970 and $345 million in 1978.[21] In 1978 there was a 49 percent increase in imports and a 22 percent increase in exports over 1977. Second, Romania's independent foreign policy stance favors increased U.S.-Romanian industrial cooperation. There is a continuing effort on the part of Romania to reduce its economic dependence on the Soviet Union. It has substantially reduced its percentage of foreign trade with the Soviet Union to the point where only 18 percent of total trade is with its neighbor. At the same time Romania has been careful to adhere to Communist party principles in its internal affairs to prevent any repeat of what happened to Czechoslovakia when it deviated from the Soviet way.

There is, of course, the matter of Romanian indebtedness to the West, as is true for most of the other Eastern European countries. In 1977 Romania's hard-currency debt to the West amounted to $3.2 billion. The ratio of debt service to exports for 1977 was 0.42, which was below the ratios for Poland and Hungary.[22] The ratio of net debt to exports for 1976 was 1.0 compared with an average of 1.6 for all Eastern European countries, 2.5 for Poland, and 1.5 for Hungary.[23] On balance, there would appear to be no particular problem with the Romanian debt. Romania is a member of the International Monetary Fund, which enables it to obtain effective coordination of Western lending policies and advice on how to base debt rescheduling, if this is necessary. Moreover, Romanian hard-currency debt to the West appears to have stabilized. This situation may be contrasted with that of Poland, where more than half of hard-currency earnings go toward repayment of its international debt. The international money market has given Romania a favorable rating among CMEA borrowers, but Western lenders may be cautious about expanding loans on anything like the scale of the past.

Other factors that could have an impact upon U.S.-Romanian industrial cooperation are the energy shortage and Romanian countertrade policies. The Soviet Union has raised oil prices for its satellites to the Organization of Petroleum Exporting Countries' levels, but Romania has oil resources. However, Romanian oil production has reportedly leveled off. Romania will probably attempt to maintain oil exports as long as it is feasible to minimize the deficit in its balance of payments. Countertrade policies could create a problem in that Romania has enforced a policy aimed at balancing its foreign trade. There is pressure on Western firms to enter into various forms of countertrade agreements. Romania demands some of the highest countertrade percentages in Eastern Europe—up to 100 percent in some reciprocal transactions. Some U.S. firms have made it a point to resist countertrade arrangements, taking the position that most Romanian products are difficult to market in the West. It is necessary to obtain countertrade goods at low enough prices and high enough quality to make them competitive, either in terms of resale or for the purpose of in-house use.

The potential for industrial cooperation appears to be the greatest in those areas where the Romanian government has placed the most emphasis under the economic plans—machine building, chemicals, metallurgy, and energy. Under the 1976-80 plan, chemical output is expected to increase 180 percent, with priority placed on the development and expansion of synthetic yarn and fiber production.[24] In the machine-building sector, plans are to produce 34 percent of total Romanian industrial output by 1980. Priority areas include machine tools, cars, trucks, and tractors. In the metallurgical sector, the plan calls for the development of a new iron-and-steel-manufacturing facility and expansion of existing facilities in the ferrous and nonferrous metallurgical industries. An interest has been expressed in industrial-cooperation arrangements with Western firms for processing copper, lead, and zinc concentrates. Priority is also given to the development of new sources of energy. There is offshore drilling for crude oil and gas. Improved fuel efficiency also enjoys priority, with construction of hydropower and thermopower stations. Agriculture requires less attention under the economic plan, even though there is low productivity as well as shortages of skilled labor in this sector.

SUMMARY

Of all the Eastern European countries, Romania appears to be the most receptive to industrial-cooperation agreements with Western firms. Recent economic plans have called for high-growth targets, which have led to rapidly increasing demands for investment goods from the West. To expedite the transfer of technology, Romania introduced joint-venture legislation in November 1972, which permitted the creation of what can be called a "transideological corporation," a corporation owned and operated by a private enterprise from the West and a state enterprise from the East. A good example of a transideological corporation is Romcontroldata, which was created by the U.S. Control Data Corporation and the Industrial Group for Electronic and Calculating Techniques of Romania. The Romanian partner contributed 55 percent of the company's capital, and the U.S. partner provided 45 percent. The contributions assumed many and varied forms, such as the building, technological equipment, assembly and testing, and technical assistance. The object of the company is to manufacture and market peripheral equipment, in particular a magnetic disk storage unit. Its products are offered for sale in both the Eastern and Western European markets, with sales contemplated in the China market.

The potential for joint ventures and other forms of industrial cooperation between Romanian and Western enterprises appears to be quite mixed. On the plus side Romania enjoys excellent economic and political contacts with the People's Republic of China and Third

World countries. Business contacts with Romania can provide an entrée into new markets in which there is considerable potential. Romania also openly courts Western firms, and its attitude toward industrial cooperation is probably the most liberal in Eastern Europe. There is high-level pressure to record as many cooperation agreements as possible. Various tax concessions are provided to encourage industrial cooperation, but the effectiveness of these concessions in attracting Western firms is difficult to prove. Entrance into the Romanian market can also provide Western firms with an entrée into other Eastern European countries. However, the potential for gain appears to be mixed. Romania's attempt to detach itself from the political influence of the Soviet Union may have an adverse effect on its relations with other Eastern European countries. On the other hand, some Western firms have expressed the view that their presence in Romania is a positive factor when it comes to doing business in Eastern Europe.

There are also some negative factors that may inhibit industrial cooperation between Romania and the West. Although much emphasis has been placed upon concluding joint-venture agreements, few have actually been consummated. There are several factors involved, the most important of which is the bureaucratic process. This process, at least in the case of Control Data, can prove to be expensive and time-consuming. Finding a mutually acceptable basis for pay scales for workers can also create problems, at least with respect to the creation of joint ventures. Wage payments plus fringe benefits can be relatively expensive, but labor costs are still lower than those that prevail in Western Europe. Wages are set under the Romanian five-year plan and will move up much more slowly than wages in the West. The technical capacity of the Romanians, particularly in the area of quality control, is inferior by Western standards. Romanian workers usually have to be trained by Western technicians to make high-quality products. Insistence on countertrade can create problems. On balance, however, the plus factors probably outweigh the negative factors, and Romania appears to provide a good opportunity for industrial cooperation on the part of Western business firms.

NOTES

1. U.S., Department of Commerce, Bureau of East-West Trade, Joint Venture Agreements in Romania (Washington, D.C.: Government Printing Office, 1977).

2. Romania, Chamber of Commerce and Industry, Guidebook on the Constitution of Joint Companies in Romania (Bucharest: Publicom, 1979).

3. All of the information used on Control Data was provided by the company.

4. This was a problem initially common to all joint ventures in Romania.

5. Telephone conversation with N. L. Dickinson, vice-president, East European/Mid East Marketing.

6. U.S., Congress, Joint Economic Committee, Issues in East-West Commercial Relations, 95th Cong., 2d sess., 1979, p. 21.

7. Business International, Solving East European Business Problems (Geneva, Switzerland: Business International, 1977), p. 98.

8. Data provided by the Romanian Embassy, Washington, D.C.

9. International Development Research Center, "Technology Transfer: Statistical Findings and Analysis" (chap. 4) (Study prepared for the Bureau of East-West Trade, U.S. Department of Commerce, Indiana University, October 1975), tables 1-3. A summary of the study can be found in Paul Marer and Joseph C. Miller, "U.S. Participation in East-West Industrial Cooperation Agreements," Journal of International Business Studies, Fall-Winter 1977, pp. 17-29.

10. International Development Research Center, "Technology Transfer," table 2.

11. Ibid., table 3.

12. In 1973 Clark Equipment Company sales totaled $1.37 billion, with overseas sales contributing in excess of one-third of this amount. Sales in Eastern Europe amounted to $3.7 million. Clark viewed this area as one of the most promising for future expansion.

13. All of the information was provided by the Clark Equipment Company.

14. Information provided by the US Steel Corporation.

15. Information provided by the Norton Company.

16. Information provided by General Tire.

17. Information provided by Occidental Petroleum.

18. Information provided by Gulf Oil.

19. Information provided by Coca-Cola.

20. Romania, Chamber of Commerce and Industry, Romania: Economic Data, 1978 (Bucharest: Publicom, 1979).

21. U.S., Congress, Joint Economic Committee, Issues in East-West Commercial Relations, p. 225.

22. Brookings Institution, Economic Relations between East and West: Prospects and Problems (Washington, D.C.: Brookings Institution, 1978), p. 23.

23. Ibid., p. 24.

24. U.S., Congress, Joint Economic Committee, East European Economies: Post-Helsinki, 95th Cong., 1st sess., August 25, 1977, p. 45.

7
THE FUTURE OF EAST-WEST INDUSTRIAL COOPERATION

During the halcyon years of détente, there was a prevailing sentiment on the part of Western business firms that the Eastern bloc countries offered unlimited market opportunities. Commercial relations between East and West expanded dramatically, with exports and imports between the United States and the East tripling during the 1970-74 period. New forms of commercial transactions also developed and were classified under the general category of industrial cooperation, which involves an economic relationship arising from contracts extending over a number of years between partners belonging to different economic systems. Industrial cooperation goes far beyond the sale or purchase of goods and services or simple export-import transactions; it involves reciprocal operations in such areas as marketing, production, and the exchange of technology. The forms of business relations that come under the category of industrial cooperation are varied in terms of arrangements that provide Western business firms with a means to penetrate socialist markets and earn an additional return on their investment in technology. Industrial-cooperation arrangements can range from simple licensing agreements to the more complex joint ventures, which involve the creation of the so-called transideological corporation.

The euphoria of détente had largely disappeared in the United States and the Soviet Union by the mid-1970s. Prospects for increased trade with the socialist countries, which once had appeared bright, diminished considerably, and many U.S. firms began to have second thoughts about doing business in the socialist markets. But East-West trade can be expected to continue to increase with or without U.S. business involvement. An expansion of trade depends on the political and legal environment in which U.S. trade with the socialist countries will take place. There is a high degree of uncertainty as to

133

what that environment will be in the future. U.S. business firms are already in a disadvantaged position in East-West trade because of their late start, and the Eastern European countries are more attuned to doing business with Western European business firms. Once channels of communication have been created, it is somewhat difficult for U.S. firms to make connections. Nevertheless, many U.S. business firms have effectively penetrated the Eastern European markets and have been successful in concluding a wide variety of industrial-cooperation agreements. There are, however, several factors that are bound to have an impact upon the potential for future industrial cooperation between Eastern and Western enterprises.

EASTERN INDEBTEDNESS TO THE WEST

During the euphoric period of détente, Western lending institutions were more than willing to make credit available to the socialist countries so that Western firms could consummate major business deals. The socialist countries, faced with a chronic shortage of hard currency, were anxious to obtain Western credit. As a result Eastern European outstanding medium- and long-term debt to the West increased steadily during the 1970s. A point has been reached where the borrowing capacities of several of the Eastern European countries are subject to some question. During the 1970-74 period, the net debt outstanding of the East to the West increased from $13 billion to $46 billion. There were several factors that contributed to the rapid rise in the debt: poor agricultural harvests, which required increased grain imports from Western sources; a recession in the West, which reduced imports from the Eastern European countries; and oil shortages, which drove up world prices of oil with a concomitant drain on the hard-currency reserves of the Eastern countries. The smaller countries of Eastern Europe—in particular Bulgaria and Poland—were the most adversely affected by an increase in the world price of oil and raw material shortages.

The Eastern European debt to the West can create some potential problems with respect to East-West relations. First, there is the possibility of default or the threat of default to gain concessions from the West. Given the magnitude of the debt, a default could have an adverse impact upon Western financial markets. However, the impact would be greater upon the debtor, for there would ensue the loss of future financial aid and the imports this aid would finance. Unless there are extreme military and political tensions, it is unlikely that any Eastern European country will default on its debt. Even in the case of the most debt-ridden country, Poland, there is always the possibility that a solution can be arranged. Despite its very high hard-currency-to-debt-service ratio, which reached 54 percent in 1978, Poland was able to obtain a seven-year Eurocurrency loan. This loan is for $500 million and is to be used to help repay maturing debt. It carries an interest spread of 1.250 percent over interbank rates for the first two years and 1.375 percent for the remaining five years.

A second problem involves Eastern ability to repay debts. Western financial institutions may have no concern over defaults but may have questions concerning credit standing and repayment of debt. When the bulk of hard-currency earnings has to go to payments of interest and amortization on Western loans, the Eastern country may experience difficulty in securing more loans. The ratio of debt services to exports is quite high in comparison with other countries of the world. A debt-service ratio of 0.25 is considered by bankers as a signal for lending caution. The ratios of all the Eastern European countries are above this ratio—ranging from a high of 0.85 in Bulgaria to a low of 0.28 in the Soviet Union. These ratios can be compared with an average ratio of 0.20 for 84 developing countries. By the same token the ratio of net debt to exports for the Eastern European countries calls into question their ability to repay debt. In 1976 the average ratio of net debt to exports for the Eastern European countries was 1.6, which was higher than the average ratio of 1.1 for 84 developing countries. The ratio of net debt to exports ranged from a high in Bulgaria of 3.3 to a low of 1.1 in the Soviet Union.

Individual Eastern European countries possess differing capacities for handling hard-currency debt. Poland is beset by economic problems, which were intensified by spring floods in 1979. These floods wreaked havoc with the agricultural sector of the Polish economy, negating any opportunity to earn additional hard currency through exports of food products. There is overemployment, generally low productivity in most industries, and an emphasis upon meeting quantity-output goals as expressed in the economic plan rather than upon stressing quality of output. But this holds true for all socialist countries. On balance, it can be said that the rapid rate of growth in debt during the mid-1970s cannot be sustained. There has to be some retrenchment, and debt rescheduling may be necessary. There is a conscious effort being made by the Eastern European countries to curtail deficits in trade by restricting unnecessary imports. Their ability to rectify trade deficits depends upon export access to Western markets, for this is the way in which hard currency can be earned to repay the debt. Import restriction and export promotion are policy choices that have to be made if the Eastern European countries are to cope successfully with their debt problems.

BARRIERS TO TRADE

Trade with the East, at least as far as the United States is concerned, is somewhat of a controversial subject. Since many business arrangements involve the sale of factories, on-site participation by U.S. companies, and the sale of finished products back to the United States as the method of payment, the arrangements have assumed many of the characteristics of U.S. investment in other parts of the world. This extension of the commercial relationship beyond simple sales transactions raises a series of difficult questions for the United States in the areas of national security and international competition. The transfer of advanced technology might be considered militarily sensitive. The United States also has to consider the possibility that the sale of know-how to the socialist countries could redound to the disadvantage of U.S. business firms. Companies that have to compete in the marketplace must continuously work at developing new products, and the development of new products must be paid for from the sales of the old. The socialist countries do not have this problem. If they are anxious to earn foreign exchange, true costs can be ignored and the product can be sold abroad below cost, enabling them to capture third-country markets at the expense of U.S. competitors.

Another impediment to U.S. trade with Eastern Europe is discriminatory tariff treatment. Even though most-favored-nation (MFN) status has been extended to Hungary, Poland, and Romania, this may not mean as much as appears on the surface. Some U.S. firms contend that MFN status really does not count for much in doing business with the socialist countries. In fact, the extension of this trading privilege to a socialist country does not mean that it will receive special privileges not received by other U.S. trading partners. To the contrary the granting of MFN status simply removes existing discrimination. Nevertheless, there are political as well as economic aspects of MFN treatment. The United States extends this treatment to some socialist countries but not to others. From the Eastern European viewpoint, nondiscriminatory tariff treatment is a desideratum in terms of trade. A continued expansion of East-West trade will require Western absorption of Eastern exports if these countries are to be able to pay for their imports. The socialist countries do not want their exports to be denied equality of treatment vis-à-vis other exports to the U.S. markets.

There are other factors that could have an effect upon U.S. economic relations with Eastern Europe. It appears essential that a successful negotiation of the Strategic Arms Limitation Treaty II be completed and implemented by the U.S. Congress as a condition for paving the way for more favorable credit and tariff treatment to be afforded to the Soviet Union. If this occurs, it is conceivable that Bulgaria, Czechoslovakia, and East Germany will obtain MFN treatment as well as Export-Import Bank credits. Then there is the human rights factor. The Jackson-Vanik Amendment to the Trade Act of 1974 conditions U.S. trading relations with the Soviet Union, China, and other socialist countries on human rights factors. If these conditions are fulfilled—and there is some evidence that they are—Congress may afford the Soviet Union favorable tariff and credit treatment. Jewish emigration from the Soviet Union has increased, which is certainly a favorable factor affecting congressional extension of trade benefits to the Soviet Union. Should these benefits be extended, one should remember that they do not place the Soviet Union or any other qualifying socialist country in a more favorable position than any other country enjoying normal trade relations with the United States.

U.S. BUSINESS VIEWS TOWARD
FUTURE INVOLVEMENT IN EASTERN EUROPE

One way to gain insight into the potential for continued U.S. industrial cooperation with Eastern Europe is to contact business firms that are actually involved in cooperation agreements. Some 40 firms responded to a questionnaire concerning their reasons for being in Eastern Europe and their views on the outlook for continued cooperation. Surprisingly, the great majority rated the potential for continued business involvement as good to fair. Only one firm rated the potential as poor. Some companies felt that the hard-currency problem was not a deterrent to industrial cooperation. As one respondent said, "If they want Western technology, they can always find a way to pay for it." However, some companies did feel that the shortage of hard currency places restrictions on continued industrial cooperation.

Plus Factors

A number of positive factors were cited as reasons for continued industrial cooperation with Eastern Europe. The senior vice-president of a large chemical company, with licensing agreements in Hungary and the Soviet Union and exports to all of the Eastern European countries, succinctly states, "They are good customers, they pay on time and have honored all of the agreements that we have negotiated with them." The shortage of hard currency, at least to this company, poses no problem, and there are no reciprocities involved, nor has there been counterpurchase pressure as a condition for doing business. The company takes a positive attitude toward Eastern European trade and has been increasing its business involvement over the years. Its licensing arrangements involve a one-time hard-currency payment for the technology, with no on-going royalty payments. An integral part of the technology is based on the company's supplying either a raw material or intermediate product to the licensee.

Other factors cited include the Eastern need for technology, relatively inexpensive production, and a desire to increase one's share of the market. An executive for a major U.S. computer firm commented, "The potential for industrial cooperation in the computer business is excellent because the Eastern Europeans vitally need technology, management assistance, etc., and they are well aware of this need." Market opportunities are cited as a major plus factor by a chemical company. With a population twice that of Western Europe and a very large industrial and agricultural output, the Eastern European countries, according to this company, represent important market opportunities. The company's purchases from Eastern Europe totaled almost $300 million in 1978. Some of the purchases were developed as part of product conversions and result in related sales to the country involved, while other purchases were based on the merit of a strong supply situation. The company proposes forms of industrial cooperation that link its planning with that of its socialist partners on a long-term basis. In a sense this cooperation becomes incorporated into the official economic planning of the socialist country involved. Industrial cooperation provides a solid basis for continued growth of the company.

Executives of several companies feel that the potential for increased industrial cooperation is good in the areas of high technology and consumer goods that are not normally available in Eastern Europe. A major U.S. producer of wearing apparel is highly optimistic about the market potential for its product, pointing to a consumer market of 390 million people. Production costs are low in comparison with Western Europe and the United States, and the demand for the product is virtually unlimited. The company is willing to enter into countertrade agreements as a vehicle through which to develop the Eastern European markets. An executive of a high-technology firm believes that the market for his firm's product will remain fairly good in the future. As loans are made, significant sales of technology will occur. However, he feels that other countries such as France, Japan, and West Germany will be more successful than the United States in developing trade with Eastern Europe. A farm machinery company also regards the future potential for its product as excellent because of the large state and collective farms in the Eastern European countries. The company produces large-capacity hay and forage harvester machines, which are sought by the large-scale operations of the state and collective farms.

Minus Factors

        Countertrade requirements are listed by a number of companies
as an inhibiting factor in doing business with the Eastern European
countries. A major U.S. airplane-manufacturing company feels that
countertrade arrangements are counterproductive. Eastern European
countries expect the U.S. company with which they are dealing to dispose of goods on a basis that is not necessarily fully competitive in a
free market. When a U.S. company enters into such an arrangement
and goods are marketed on a semiforced basis, the normal business
relations necessary to continue trade are not established. The company cites its own experience in countertrade as a disappointment.
In one situation a business arrangement was canceled with an Eastern
European country when the company found that there were substantial
costs associated with countertrade. The only feasible way to handle
countertrade was through a third-party trading company. This company required a spread of 10 to 20 percent of the value of the goods
sold in hard-currency countries, depending on the goods to be sold.
In another situation the company found it difficult to dispose of Eastern European goods in the U.S. markets, with the exception of a
limited amount of goods it could take for its own use.

        To some firms countertrade does not present an obstacle in
dealing with the Eastern European countries. An executive of an electronic firm says, "Quid pro quo may be the way to go." His company
is quite willing to consider countertrade arrangements, particularly
in those countries where there is a lack of hard currency. A farm
equipment company feels that the potential for doing business in the
Eastern European countries is in direct proportion to the potential
it has for making counterpurchases in those countries. Its main
countertrade arrangements have been with Bulgaria, Hungary, and
Romania, but it is willing to consider some form of countertrade in
every country in which it deals. An industrial equipment company
also is satisfied with countertrade agreements. It has successfully
completed a countertrade agreement it had with Romania and feels
that the potential for continued business involvement in Eastern Europe is particularly good in Hungary, Poland, and Romania but not
so encouraging in the other countries.

        Hard-currency limitations are cited by a number of U.S. firms
as a problem that will continue to affect business involvement in Eastern Europe. An executive of a consumer goods firm suggests, "At
the present time, the potential for business involvement in Eastern
European countries is not too good in our opinion because of the hard
currency limitation and the limitation of products and commodities for
export which could substitute for hard currency as payment." An
executive of another U.S. company feels the potential for business

involvement in Eastern Europe to be very limited by lack of hard currency. However, other firms are more sanguine about the hard-currency problem. They maintain that the necessary hard currency is available for things that are needed, particularly technology that is not available in Eastern Europe. There is also the feeling that hard-currency indebtedness creates problems for some Eastern European countries but not for others. From the standpoint of the Eastern Europeans, the major purpose of industrial-cooperation agreements is to lead toward investment that will ease their balance-of-payments problems in the future.

Other problems were also cited. In making reference to a turn-key project, the president of one firm states, "As to whether there were any difficulties in construction and operation, I'm afraid one book wouldn't cover them all." Reference is made to the fact that all but the very basic materials had to be imported, as did a great deal of skilled labor. Controls, logistics, the handling of shortages, and all the myriad considerations that are relatively simple on a domestic project turned out to be major problems. There is concern on the part of an executive of a large U.S. construction company that U.S. technology will be used as a weapon against U.S. firms. In his opinion most of the Eastern European countries are looking for technical know-how to incorporate into their own production, meaning that they will eventually compete against Western firms. They can set their own prices regardless of cost, so competing with the West on a price-comparison basis presents no problem. This is true up to a point; however, no matter how technically perfect the product, the socialist countries are notoriously deficient in managerial and marketing skills. It is one thing to produce a product; it is something else to distribute it.

Types of U.S. Firms Involved

The majority of U.S. firms polled would qualify as multinational corporations by any standard. Many would also qualify as leaders in their respective industries and have operating divisions in Western Europe, expediting access to Eastern Europe. They represent a wide range of industries—automotive, aluminum, chemicals, computers, farm machinery, glass, electronic, aircraft, pharmaceuticals, heavy equipment, steel, and machine tools. However, there are some firms that are small and would not be considered multinational corporations. They are specialized in nature and deal with specific products that may be in demand in Eastern Europe. An example is the construction of a turnkey meat-packing plant. Usually there is a one-shot arrangement; once the project is completed, that is it. Industrial cooperation involves a long-term arrangement for many of the larger U.S. firms. Dow Chemical concluded a ten-year cooperation agreement with Poland involving major purchase and supply commitments, including exports to Dow that provide financing for new plant facilities in Poland. In 1978 total trade between Dow and Poland reached almost $50 million and involved 50 different products. In 1973 Dow received accreditation from the Polish government for a commercial representation office—the first such accreditation given to any foreign firm.

The sharing of proceeds varies considerably among the U.S. firms. A chemical company licensed its processes and in each instance received a one-time payment for the technology with no ongoing royalty payments. Singer has an agreement with Poland that licenses it to produce a particular household sewing machine using Singer's designs, patents, trademarks, and know-how. A portion of these machines is sold in the Comecon area, and Singer purchases machines for distribution in Western countries. The company received an engineering fee at the start of the licensing agreement and continues to receive a royalty on each machine produced. Another U.S. firm has a licensing agreement with Romania to manufacture transmissions. It charges a disclosure fee and agrees to counterpurchase sufficient products to cover at least a part of the fee. A clothing company receives a royalty payment for each garment produced and sold in Hungary and, in addition, receives the garments for resale at attractive prices. A number of firms have some sort of countertrade arrangement, including a barter deal. One firm regards countertrade as desirable as a means of gaining access to the Eastern European markets. Other firms reject countertrade as a matter of policy. Apparently, sharing arrangements depend on negotiations between the individual company and country involved in the cooperation agreement.

EASTERN EUROPEAN PROBLEMS

Eastern European countries must come to grips with their external debt problems. A continued supply of financing from the West is necessary for maintaining trade levels. However, there are other problems that also have some impact upon industrial cooperation. One is product quality, which makes countertrade undesirable in many cases, because the Western firm cannot market the Eastern product. Greater attention as well as investment should go into packaging from an appearance standpoint. There are no quality control standards for many products, and replacement parts are often nonexistent. In manufactured products destined for countertrade, frequently the Western partner refuses to accept or dispose of products that are of poor quality. When the Western partner attempts to negotiate certain changes or improvements to make the product more salable, delays occur that lengthen the delivery time, or there is a new contract that often calls for an increase in the size of the counterpurchase. There is also the need for incorporating fashionable designs and features into products sold in foreign markets.

Introducing innovative technology and products is a very difficult task for the Eastern European countries. The technology available to produce goods for export has in many cases been bought from the West. This "new" technology is in many cases "old" in terms of Western standards. The most advanced technology of the West is usually not made available to the Eastern European countries for various reasons, including national security interests and a desire by some firms to prevent the East from copying their best technology. But the Eastern European countries appear to have difficulty in absorbing advanced technology. The products that are being exported by the East have in most cases reached maturity in the product life cycle. This means that they have to penetrate Western markets that are already saturated. It is quite difficult to improve the performance of products in the advanced stage of the life cycle without further investments in new technology or the capacity to develop new innovations. The deleterious effects of the combination of manufacturing technology that is old by Western standards and products that are at the end of the maturity stage of the life cycle are further compounded by the frequent inability of Eastern enterprises to adjust to changes in export demand.

Another area for concern is the lack of managers trained in a competitive market environment. Traditional Eastern European exports, such as raw materials, do not require as much marketing expertise as manufactured exports require. Moreover, manufactured products need sophisticated market research techniques and large capital outlays for promotion, distribution, and service. There appears to be a broad endorsement by Eastern European governments of the idea of increased managerial responsibility, while at the same time they want to increase their power to subordinate and monitor the decisions of managers in the areas of investment, marketing, and efficiency. All the Eastern European countries state that more qualified managers must be hired, that they must be more effective, and that they must assume more responsibility for their actions and decisions. But this runs counter to actuality, and in the final analysis, managers have little power because of the various conditions and constraints placed on them. The Eastern European countries have problems in the basic areas of motivation, responsibility, and rewards for managers.

SUMMARY

The potential for increased U.S. business involvement in Eastern Europe appears to be mixed. Favorable factors from the U.S. standpoint include the opportunity to increase market shares or extend markets, the large population of Eastern Europe, and the need for Western technology. The major limiting factor is Eastern hard-currency indebtedness to the West. There is also some feeling on the part of U.S. firms that countertrade and licensing are counterproductive, the first because it is not competitive, and the second because it may create competition against U.S. products. But there are certain handicaps common to centrally planned economic systems that limit competitive potential. There are difficulties with the quality of products. The centralization of resource allocation decisions, the prevalence of a domestic seller's market, and a lack of managerial and marketing expertise all combine to limit production of goods that would be most salable in Western markets. Incentives for technical change are weak; yet much of the competition in international markets, particulary in manufacturing, depends on product innovation, an area in which the centrally planned economies are very weak. The poor connection between realized foreign-trade prices and success indicators discourages Eastern producers from making the efforts required to develop and market goods in the West.

In a broader perspective that involves both business and government, there are those persons who view East-West trade as mutually advantageous and project an expanding long-term market for Western products. For U.S. firms this would mean profit and would keep costs down by permitting economies of scale resulting from increased production. There is also the feeling that world stability will be promoted by increased economic cooperation between East and West and that economic interdependence will cause a shift away from military concerns. Conversely, there are those persons, particularly within the U.S. Congress, who feel that few benefits will accrue to the United States from an expansion of trade with Eastern Europe. For them trade is a one-way street in terms of benefits: the Eastern European countries are the beneficiaries because they gain valuable technology that can be used to the economic and military detriment of the United States. The cost to the United States outweighs the benefits to be gained from increased trade. Moreover, since the volume of Eastern European trade is small in relation to total U.S. trade, it is felt that the benefits to U.S. firms and to the economy as a whole are limited.

Congressional views toward trade with the East—as reflected in the Export Administration Amendments of 1977—could have a significant impact on the future of East-West trade. This law is aimed at improving export-licensing procedures. The secretary of commerce is required to either act on an export-licensing application within 90 days or inform an applicant in writing of the reasons for any delay. If no action is taken within 90 days, the license is automatic. The law also states that in administering export controls for national security purposes, U.S. policy toward a country cannot be determined exclusively on the basis of whether it is Communist or non-Communist. The policy should take into account the country's present and potential relationship with the United States and its present and potential relationship with countries friendly and hostile to the United States. The law, however, directs the secretary of defense to recommend a restriction on the export of goods and technology that would make a significant contribution to the military potential of any country if it would prove detrimental to the national security of the United States. Control Data, for example, was denied a license to export the Cyber-76 computer to the Soviet Union.

Deteriorating U.S.-Soviet relations, exacerbated by the Afghanistan conflict, are bound to have an adverse impact on East-West trade. However, even before Afghanistan, the Eastern European countries were in economic and political trouble because of flagging growth rates, inflation, shortages, and rising oil bills. The immediate future looks bleak, particulary with no improvement in U.S.-Soviet relations foreseen in the immediate future. The debt of the East to Western lenders has increased, with Poland heading toward a $20 billion debt to the West by the end of 1980. Faced with internal and external economic pressures, Eastern European policy makers will have to continue to keep tight limits on imports and to look for new ways to boost exports. This means that industrial-cooperation agreements with the West will probably continue to be more selective as loans from the West will be harder to obtain. It might be added, however, that Western European firms are less likely to be affected by the cold war fallout between Washington and Moscow than U.S. firms. The French have pretty much served notice that what happens between Washington and Moscow over Afghanistan and the Olympics will have no effect on French commercial relations with Eastern Europe.

Improving U.S. relations with the People's Republic of China may also have an impact on continued industrial-cooperation agreements with Eastern Europe. A new Chinese joint-venture law provides a framework for U.S. and other Western investors to do business in China. It provides for the establishment of limited-liability companies between Chinese entities and foreign corporations on the basis of "equality and mutual benefit." The law specifies that foreign participation must constitute at least 25 percent of the venture and that the chairperson of the venture must be Chinese. The venture law is regarded as a favorable omen by Western business firms because it indicates that the Chinese place value on Western involvement in their process of modernization. It marks a departure from ideology and politics to concrete economic issues of the present. The new law and the persistent perception of China as a vast new market ready to be sold Pepsi-Colas and Marlboros creates interest on the part of Western investors. China has also maintained an excellent international credit rating. Balanced against these factors is China's frequent radical shifts in ideology over the last 30 years, a factor that could affect interest in investing in long-term projects.

SELECTED BIBLIOGRAPHY

BOOKS

Atlantic Council. Committee on East-West Trade. East-West Trade: Managing, Encounter, and Accommodation. Boulder, Colo.: Westview Press, 1977.

Ausch, Sandor. Theory and Practice of CMEA Cooperation. Budapest: Academic Publishing House, 1972.

Barnet, Richard J., and Ronald E. Muller. Global Reach: The Power of the Multinational Corporations. New York: Simon and Schuster, 1974.

Basche, James R. Evolving Corporate Policy and Organization for East-West Trade. New York: Conference Board, 1975.

Brookings Institution. Economic Relations between East and West: Prospects and Problems. Washington, D.C.: Brookings Institution, 1978.

Business International. Solving East European Business Problems. Geneva, Switzerland: Business International, 1977.

Carleton University. East-West Project. Directory of Soviet and East European Companies in the West. Ottawa, 1978.

Czepurko, Aleksander. East-West Trade Prospects up to 1980. Vienna: Weiner Institut für Internationale Wirtschaftsvergleiche, 1976.

Friesen, Connie M. The Political Economy of East-West Trade. New York: Praeger, 1976.

Goldman, Marshall. Détente and Dollars. New York: Basic Books, 1976.

Kindleberger, Charles P. American Business Abroad: Six Lectures on Direct Investment. New Haven, Conn.: Yale University Press, 1969.

Kretschmar, Robert S., and Robin Foor. The Potential for Joint Ventures in Eastern Europe. New York: Praeger, 1972.

Lauter, Geza, and Paul M. Dickie. Multinational Corporations and Eastern European Socialist Economies. New York: Praeger, 1975.

Levcik, Friedrich, and Jan Stankovsky. Industrial Cooperation between East and West. White Plains, N.Y.: M. E. Sharpe, 1979.

Levine, Herbert. Transfer of U.S. Technology to the Soviet Union: Impact of U.S. Commercial Interests. Palo Alto, Calif.: Stanford, 1975.

Levinson, Charles. Vodka Cola. London: Gordon and Cremonesi, 1979.

Marer, Paul, ed. U.S. Financing of East-West Trade: The Political Economy of Government Credits and the National Interest. Bloomington: Indiana University Press, 1975.

McMillan, Carl H., ed. Changing Perspectives in East-West Commerce. Lexington, Mass.: G. D. Heath, 1974.

McMillan, Carl, and D. P. St. Charles. Joint Ventures in Eastern Europe: A Three-Country Comparison. Montreal: C. D. Howe Research Institute, 1974.

Prasad, S. Benjamin, and Y. Krishna Shetty. An Introduction to Multinational Management. Englewood Cliffs, N.J.: Prentice-Hall, 1976.

Price Waterhouse. East-West Trade. New York: Price Waterhouse, 1978.

Rodriguez, Rita M., and E. Eugene Carter. International Financial Management. Englewood Cliffs, N.J.: Prentice-Hall, 1976.

Ryans, John K., ed. The Multinational Business World of the 1980's. Kent, Ohio: Kent State University Press, 1974.

Saunders, Christopher, ed. East-West Cooperation in Business. Vienna: Vienna Institute for Comparative Economic Studies, 1977.

Selucky, Radoslav. Economic Reforms in Eastern Europe: Political Background and Economic Significance. New York: Praeger, 1972.

Stanford Research Institute, International Strategic Studies Center. The Role of U.S.-Soviet Trade in Soviet Growth Strategy for the Seventies. Menlo Park, Calif., July 1976.

Starr, Robert, ed. East-West Business Transactions. New York: Praeger, 1974.

Trzeciakowski, Witold. "Foreign Trade Planning and Management in Poland." Warsaw: Central School of Planning and Statistics, 1973.

Turner, Louis. Multinational Corporations and the Third World. New York: Hill & Wang, 1973.

Vernon, Raymond, and Louis T. Wells. Manager in the International Economy. 3rd ed. Englewood Cliffs, N.J.: Prentice-Hall, 1976.

Wilczynski, Josef. The Multinationals and East-West Relations. London: Macmillan, 1976.

Wolf, Thomas A. "East-West Economic Relations and the Multinational Corporation." Occasional Paper no. 5. Washington, D.C.: Center for Multinational Studies, 1973.

_____. U.S. East-West Trade Policy: Economic Warfare vs. Economic Welfare. Lexington, Mass.: G. D. Heath, 1973.

JOURNAL ARTICLES AND NEWSPAPERS

Baranson, Jack. "Technology Transfer through the International Firm." American Economic Review, May 1970, pp. 435-40.

Buky, Barnabas. "Hungary on a Treadmill." Problems of Communism, September-October 1972, pp. 31-39.

"Capitalistic Troubles for Eastern Europe." Business Week, August 13, 1979, pp. 40-58.

Chandler, Margaret K. "Project Management in the Socialist Bloc." Columbia Journal of World Business, Summer 1978, pp. 71-86.

"Complex Form of Sharing, Control Data, Romania Own Computer Plant." Washington Post, December 5, 1976.

"Do's and Don't's of Landing a Polish Contract." Forbes, July 1, 1977, p. 46.

"East-West Joint Ventures Increase." World Business, September 3, 1979, p. 27.

"East-West Trade Expansion Push in the New Congress." East-West Trade Council, January 15, 1979.

"Foreign Trade: Barter Is Back, Bigger than Ever." U.S. News and World Reports, December 3, 1979, pp. 95-96.

Grabowski, Jan, and Eugeniusz Tabaczynski. "East-West International Investment and Production Ventures." Handel Jagraniczny 19 (1974): 8-14.

Holt, John B. "Industrial Cooperation in Eastern Europe: Strategies of U.S. Agricultural and Construction Equipment Companies." Columbia Journal of World Business, Spring 1977, pp. 80-89.

Horbaczewski, Henry Z. "Profitable Coexistence: The Legal Foundation for Joint Enterprises with U.S. Participation in Poland." Business Lawyer 31 (November 1975): 433-55.

Lamm, L. J. "Technology Exchange with the CMEA Countries." East-West Technology Digest, November 1976, pp. 80-88.

Lauter, Geza P., and Paul M. Dickie. "Multinational Corporations in Eastern European Socialist Economies." Journal of Marketing, October 1975, pp. 40-46.

Mandato, Joseph, Thomas J. Skola, and Kenneth L. Wyse. "Counterpurchase Sales in the German Democratic Republic." Columbia Journal of World Business, Spring 1978, pp. 82-88.

Marer, Paul, and Joseph C. Miller. "U.S. Participation in East-West Industrial Cooperation Agreements." Journal of International Business Studies, Fall-Winter 1979, pp. 17-29.

"Multinationals: Russia Takes the Plunge." U.S. News and World Reports, February 20, 1978, pp. 52-53.

"Poland: Huge Debt Stalls Western Ventures." Business Week, January 17, 1977, pp. 18-19.

Quinn, James B. "Technology Transfer by Multinational Companies." Harvard Business Review, November-December 1969, pp. 147-61.

"Romania: Maverick Among Eastern Traders." Advertising Age, January 9, 1978, p. 46.

"Sharply Rising Prices, Other Economic Woes Plague Eastern Europe." Wall Street Journal, November 29, 1979, pp. 40-41.

"U.S.-Hungarian Trade Agreement Initiated: Has Tariff Reciprocity." Commerce America, March 13, 1978, p. 10.

Vernon, Raymond. "International Investment and International Trade in the Product Life Cycle." Quarterly Journal of Economics 80 (1966): 190-207.

GOVERNMENT PUBLICATIONS

United States

Central Intelligence Agency, National Foreign Assessment Center. The Scope of Poland's Economic Dilemma. Washington, D.C.: U.S. Government Printing Office, July 1978.

_____. Soviet Economic Problems and Prospects. Washington, D.C.: U.S. Government Printing Office, July 1977.

International Trade Commission. 17th Quarterly Report to the Congress and the East-West Foreign Trade Board on Trade between the United States and the Nonmarket Economy Countries. Washington, D.C.: U.S. Government Printing Office, February 1979.

_____. Special Report on Probable Impact on U.S. Trade of Granting MFN Treatment to the U.S.S.R. Washington, D.C.: U.S. Government Printing Office, n.d.

U.S., Congress. Joint Economic Committee. East European Economies: Post-Helsinki, 95th Cong., 1st sess., August 25, 1977.

_____. Issues in East-West Commercial Relations, 95th Cong., 2d sess., 1979.

_____. Technology, Economic Growth, and International Competitiveness: Report Prepared for Subcommittee on Economic Growth, 94th Cong., 1st sess., 1975.

U.S., Congress, Senate. Committee on Finance. Implications of Multinational Firms for World Trade and Investment and for U.S. Trade and Labor: Report to the Subcommittee on International Trade, 93rd Cong., 1st sess., 1973, pp. 80-83.

U.S., Congress, Senate. Committee on Foreign Relations. U.S. Trade and Investment in the Soviet Union and Eastern Europe: Staff Report for the Subcommittee on Multinational Corporations, 93rd Cong., 2d sess., 1974.

U.S., Department of Commerce. East-West Countertrade Practices. Washington, D.C.: Government Printing Office, 1978.

_____. The United States Role in East-West Trade: Problems and Prospects. Washington, D.C.: Government Printing Office, August 1975.

U.S., Department of Defense. Long-Range U.S.-U.S.S.R. Competition: National Security Implications. National Security Affairs Conference. Washington, D.C.: Government Printing Office, 1976.

U.S., Department of State. Report on the Potential for Technology Transfer from the Soviet Union to the United States. Washington, D.C.: Government Printing Office, July 1977.

Other Countries

Federal Republic of West Germany, Bundesministerium für Wirtschaft. Der Deutsche Osthandel zu Beginn des Jahres 1977. Bonn, 1977.

Organization for Economic Cooperation and Development. Technology Transfer between East and West. September 1977.

Romania, Chamber of Commerce and Industry. Guidebook on the Constitution of Joint Companies in Romania. Bucharest: Publicom, 1979.

_____. Romanian Foreign Trade Law. Bucharest: Publicom, 1978.

Romania, Foreign Trade Agency. Doing Business with Romania: Opportunities for U.S. Businessmen. Bucharest: Publicom, 1979.

_____. Your Commercial Partners in Romania. Bucharest: Publicom, 1979.

INDEX

ABOUT THE AUTHOR

MARTIN SCHNITZER is Professor of Business in the College of Business Adminstration at Virginia Polytechnic Institute and State University. He serves as an economic adviser to the governor of Virginia and has served as a member of a presidential task force on welfare reform. He also served as a member of the U.S. East-West Advisory Board and as an adviser to the U.S. secretary of commerce.

Dr. Schnitzer is a past editor of the Virginia Social Science Journal and has published a number of articles and books, including Comparative Economic Systems and Contemporary Government and Business Relations. He is the author of several Praeger Special Series titles: Regional Unemployment and the Relocation of Workers, The Economy of Sweden, East and West Germany, and Income Distribution.

Dr. Schnitzer earned his Ph.D. in economics at the University of Florida, has done advanced work at summer institutes at Harvard Business School and the University of Virginia, and has been the beneficiary of grants for research work abroad.